OTHER VOLUMES IN
EXERCISES IN DIAGNOSTIC RADIOLOGY

Published

Forthcoming

EXERCISES IN DIAGNOSTIC RADIOLOGY

7

THE EMERGENCY PATIENT

CHARLES S. LANGSTON, M.D.

Instructor in Radiology, Harvard Medical
School; Radiologist, Mount Auburn Hospital,
Cambridge, Massachusetts; Formerly, Assistant
in Radiology, Massachusetts General Hospital,
Boston, Massachusetts

LUCY FRANK SQUIRE, M.D.

Professor of Radiology, Downstate Medical
Center, Brooklyn, New York; Consultant in
Radiology, Massachusetts General Hospital,
Boston, Massachusetts

W. B. SAUNDERS COMPANY · PHILADELPHIA · LONDON · TORONTO   1975

W. B. Saunders Company: West Washington Square
Philadelphia, PA   19105

12 Dyott Street
London, WC1A   1DB

833 Oxford Street
Toronto, Ontario M8Z   5T9, Canada

Library of Congress Cataloging in Publication Data (Revised)

Squire, Lucy Frank.

Exercises in diagnostic radiology.

CONTENTS: 1. The chest. — 2. The abdomen — 3. Bone. [etc.]

1. Diagnosis, Radioscopic.   I. Colaiace, William M., 1938–
II. Strutynsky, Natalie, 1934–   III. Langston, C. S. IV.
Title.

RC78.S68   616.07′572   74–113034

ISBN 0–7216–5627–7

Exercises in Diagnostic Radiology — Volume 7   The Emergency Patient   ISBN 0-7216-5627 -7

Last digit is the print number: 9   8   7   6   5   4   3   2   1

PREFACE

Nowhere in medicine is the skill and judgment of a good clinician more important than in the Emergency Room. He must act quickly and effectively, sometimes with only a minimum of history and a quick physical examination. Laboratory data are often limited. In this situation emergency radiologic examinations have become an increasingly important adjunct to the history and physical examination.

Since the attending clinician often has only a few symptoms or signs to go on when he refers his patient to the radiologist, we have chosen to organize our cases according to chief complaint, such as chest pain, headache, shortness of breath, and so on. This is the way emergency patients usually present to the clinician and are presented to the radiologist.

The patients are real, with changed names, but with no substantive alteration in the facts of their histories. Use the clinical information. We have attempted to present the patients as they presented in reality. In most cases the pertinent "negatives" of the history have been given. Sometimes, for the sake of brevity, they have not. The reader should assume that no pertinent information has been withheld and that unusual or atypical cases will be labeled as such.

We have not attempted to present a complete spectrum of the problems which will be seen in an Emergency Room, but we do think our patients represent the majority of the emergency problems with which medical student and house officer must become familiar.

C.S.L.
L.F.S.

Charles S. Langston
Mount Auburn Hospital
Cambridge, Massachusetts 02138

ACKNOWLEDGMENTS

This volume, like so many of the *Exercises,* is an outgrowth of radiologic seminars designed for the medical students and residents at the Massachusetts General Hospital. Without their enthusiasm and, more important, their questions, it would not have been written. Credit must also be given to our many medical and surgical colleagues who helped us review some of the difficult clinical material.

Figure 147C was kindly lent by Dr. K. Sang Oh of Johns Hopkins Medical Center. Figures 96A, 101A, 104A, 112A, and 116A are drawn after illustrations in DePalma's *Fractures and Dislocations.* Figures 118B and 127D are drawn after illustrations from *Radiologic Clinics of North America,* Vol. 4, No. 2.

We would also like to thank Miss Florence Campfiore and Miss July Belli for their help in typing and reading the manuscript, and Mr. Raymond Sprague for much of the photographic work.

CHARLES S. LANGSTON, M.D.

CONTENTS

CONTENTS

SECTION III FEVER AND COUGH

SECTION IV HEMOPTYSIS

SECTION V ABDOMINAL PAIN

SECTION VI ABDOMINAL PAIN AND HYPOTENSION OR SHOCK

CONTENTS

CONTENTS

CONTENTS

CONTENTS

SECTION XVIII   BLUNT TRAUMA

SECTION XIX   HEADACHE

SECTION XX   HEAD TRAUMA AND COMA

SECTION I

Chest Pain

Pains in the chest cause a great many patients to come to the Emergency Room. This is in large part because the public knows about heart attacks and about angina pectoris. However, there are many causes of chest pain other than myocardial ischemia. Irritation or damage to the pericardium, pleura, tracheobronchial tree, ribs, intercostal nerves and muscles, diaphragm, aorta, esophagus, or dorsal spine may all cause pain which mimics angina.

The cause of chest pain can often be elucidated by a careful history. Pleural pain is "catching" and related to breathing; tracheal pain is deep and induced by coughing; pericardial pain may be central and influenced by position; rib and chest wall pain is usually associated with focal tenderness. These points are useful in the clinic and they may be critical in an Emergency Room. However, the patient may be too sick to give a complete history, or there may have been no previous episodes of pain. In situations like these, the radiograph becomes very useful. A chest radiograph cannot, of course, "rule out an M.I." but it may give a clue to additional or alternative diagnoses.

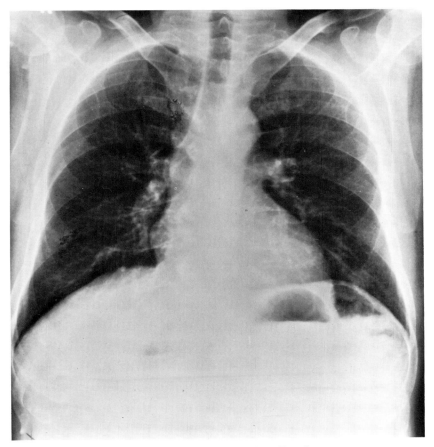

Figure 1 A   Eldridge Drudge

CASE 1 SUDDEN CHEST PAIN

Eldridge Drudge is a 47-year-old book-keeper who comes to the Emergency Room because he suddenly developed a squeezing pain in the chest while working this morning. He felt weak and nauseated, but he finished the day's work. The pain has not returned. Mr. Drudge is a quiet man who has been in good health all his life. He had a checkup a year ago including a cardiogram which was said to be normal. He has smoked cigarettes for years but now smokes only a pipe.

Eldridge looks nervous but otherwise well. His vital signs are blood pressure 136/92, pulse 74, respiration 14, and temperature 98.6° (po). His cardiorespiratory examination is normal: the lungs are clear and the heart sounds are strong. The EKG shows ST segment elevation in leads I, AVL, and V6 but is otherwise normal.

You send him for a chest film with a diagnosis "rule out M.I." What do you make of the films? What other diagnostic possibilities would you expect the radiologist to consider on the basis of your requisition?

ANSWER

Well, this is a normal chest film. The lungs are well and symmetrically aerated. The heart is normal in size and shape. Mr. Drudge has suffered myocardial infarction; but the diagnosis was made by serial EKG's and enzymes, not by the chest film.

What then should the radiologist be looking for on the basis of your requisition? One of the most difficult problems is differentiating patients with angina pectoris without infarction from those with infarction. The chest film is not usually of any help in this. There are, however, other diseases mimicking myocardial infarction which may have a characteristic radiologic appearance: pulmonary embolism, pericarditis with effusion, aortic aneurysm, pneumothorax, chest wall disease, and, less commonly, subdiaphragmatic diseases such as cholelithiasis, pancreatitis, or perforated duodenal ulcer. The latter causes of chest pain may be real diagnostic possibilities in an older patient in shock.

The radiologist should also look for the complications of myocardial infarction: pulmonary edema (50% of patients will develop this complication), ventricular aneurysm, mitral regurgitation (if the papillary muscle is involved in the infarct), or pulmonary emboli. He should note the presence or absence of pre-existing disease such as chronic obstructive lung disease and the position of the tip of a central venous catheter or an endotracheal tube, if these have been introduced.

CASE 2 CHEST PAIN AND SLIGHT SHORTNESS OF BREATH

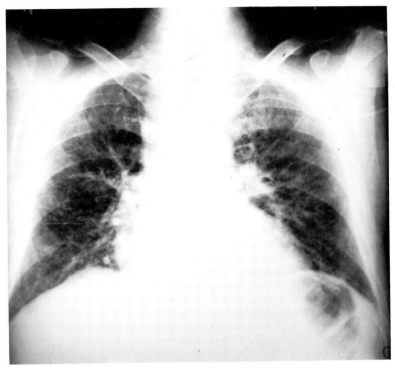

Figure 2 A   Pulling's chest film

Mr. Arthur Pulling is a 47-year-old account executive who experienced sudden crushing chest pain while seated at his desk contemplating his stock portfolio. The pain radiated to his neck and left shoulder and persisted even though he lay down on the sofa in his office. He was brought to the Emergency Room in a taxi by his secretary. Until now he has been in good health. His vital signs are blood pressure 134/86, pulse 80, respiration 20, and temperature 98.4° (po).

Mr. Pulling is anxious and slightly sweaty, though his skin is cool. He says the pain is going away, but he is nauseated and slightly short of breath. His chest is clear except for a few wheezes and a few coarse rales at the bases which do not clear with coughing. His heart sounds are normal except for occasional ventricular premature beats. The EKG shows an acute anterolateral myocardial infarction. This is an upright portable chest film (Fig. 2A) and two magnified views of the lung periphery (Figs. 2B and C, page 6). Can you make a diagnosis?

ANSWER

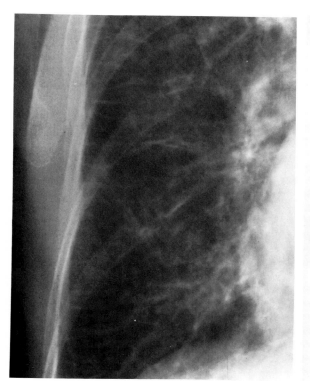

Figure 2 B   Blowup of lung periphery

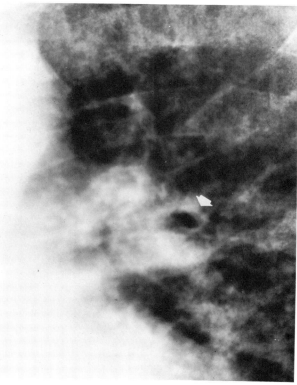

Figure 2 C   Blowup of left hilus and bronchus

Allowing for portable technique and the short tube film distance which tend to magnify cardiac size, this heart is roughly normal in size and shape. The lungs are well-expanded and there is not much respiratory motion (the diaphragm is sharp). Nevertheless, the pulmonary vascular margins are indistinct, the minor fissure is thickened, and, on the blowup, there are Kerley B lines in the periphery and fluid around a bronchus seen end on (arrow). These are all manifestations of accumulation of edema fluid in the interstitium and lymphatics of the lung. This is referred to as interstitial pulmonary edema.

When the fluid is truly interstitial, it is rare to hear bubbly rales though there may be wheezing and dyspnea. We do not understand the dyspnea. It may be related to the decreased pulmonary compliance caused by the interstitial fluid.

Mr. Pulling has had an acute myocardial infarction with occasional aberrant ventricular beats and evidence of congestive heart failure. He should be on a cardiac monitor.

CASE 3 PLEURITIC CHEST PAIN

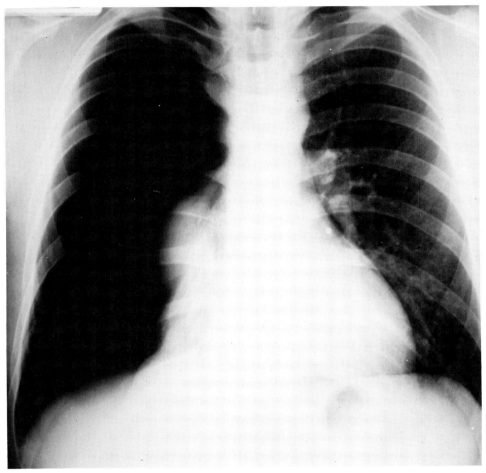

Figure 3   Alfred Burst

Alfred Burst, a 32-year-old physician/man-about-town, noted transient pleuritic chest pain following strenuous nocturnal exercise. The next morning he felt slightly dyspneic and stopped by the Emergency Room for a chest film. Here it is. What is his problem?

ANSWER

Clearly, Alfred has a large right pneumothorax with complete collapse of the right lung against the mediastinum. If he had listened to his own chest, he would have heard no breath sounds on the right. It may seem odd that such a large pneumothorax would be relatively asymptomatic, but this is often the case. It has been determined experimentally that a large pneumothorax is accompanied by a transient fall in the PO_2 which does not correct itself when 100% oxygen is administered, and which is probably due to a reduction in ventilation greater than the reduction in perfusion of the involved lung. However, in a matter of hours this "shunt" corrects itself, probably owing to a further reduction in blood flow through the collapsed lung.

Air in the pleural space is reabsorbed only slowly. For this reason it is necessary either to insert a chest tube or to aspirate the air with a syringe unless the pneumothorax is small.

The fairly common spontaneous pneumothoraces in young men are probably due to the rupture of subpleural (often apical) blebs. They may recur once or twice, but usually not more than that. Spontaneous pneumothoraces rarely require surgical intervention, although one as large as Dr. Burst's will need a chest tube. Sometimes a patient with a small pneumothorax does not even need to be hospitalized. Patients with bilateral pneumothoraces (or history of a pneumothorax on the other side) and tension pneumothoraces should be treated as real or potential emergencies, of course.

CASE 4   PLEURITIC CHEST PAIN AND SHORTNESS
OF BREATH

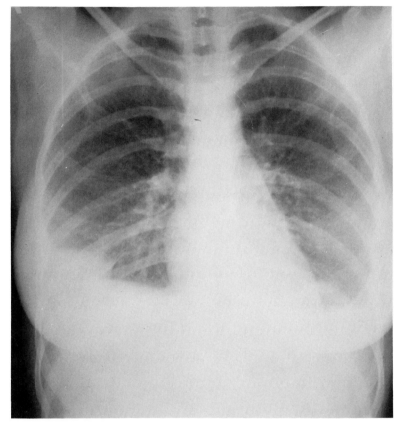

Figure 4   A   Peach Melba

Peach Melba is a 23-year-old exotic dancer (a friend of Dr. Burst) who developed sudden right pleuritic chest pain and shortness of breath while in rehearsal yesterday. She does not feel much better today and has a low-grade fever. Ms. Melba is taking birth control pills but no other medicine and is in good health.

She is a healthy looking girl who clearly avoids taking a deep breath when you examine her. Her temperature is 99.8° (po), pulse 80, respiration 25 and shallow, blood pressure 115/70. There is a coarse friction rub on the right, but the rest of the examination is normal. There is no evidence of phlebitis. Here is her chest film (Fig. 4A, PA view only). What is your tentative diagnosis? How will you confirm it?

ANSWER

This is a good picture for pulmonary embolism with infarction. There is a wedge-shaped density in the right costophrenic angle and bilateral small pleural effusions (visible only on the left because of the infarct on the right). The heart and lungs are otherwise normal. A lung scan may help.

Since you can be reasonably sure the pulmonary capillary bed in this previously healthy girl should be anatomically normal, it will be safe to conclude that defects in a radioisotope perfusion scan are due to pulmonary emboli. This assumption will only be true for the parts of the lung which are radiographically normal. Defects at the bases could be due to the pleural fluid. There will be a defect in the right costophrenic angle whether the density there is due to an infarct, hemorrhage, or pneumonia. But any defect in the areas of the lung which are normal on the chest film are supportive evidence for your diagnosis of pulmonary emboli. Here is the scan (Fig. 4B). Are you correct?

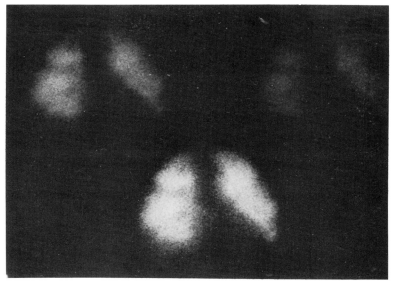

Figure 4 B   Ms. Melba's scan (frontal projection with three intensities)

Yes, there are defects throughout both lungs. Presumably there was a shower of emboli, or a single embolus which fragmented, showering small clots throughout the lung. Collateral circulation has saved most of the lung from visible infarction.

CASE 5   SEIZURE, SYNCOPE, AND LEFT CHEST PAIN

This **Unknown White Male** was found collapsed and unconscious in an alley. He was brought to the Emergency Room by the police who tell you that he had a convulsion in the wagon on the way to the hospital. You find him to be a middle-aged man dressed in work clothes, but with no identification. He has the faint odor of alcohol on his breath. He is now confused and somnolent, but otherwise neurologically intact. When aroused, he says he has pain on the left side of his chest. His vital signs are normal as are his cardiorespiratory exam and his EKG. This is his portable chest film (Fig. 5). Do you think he has had a heart attack?

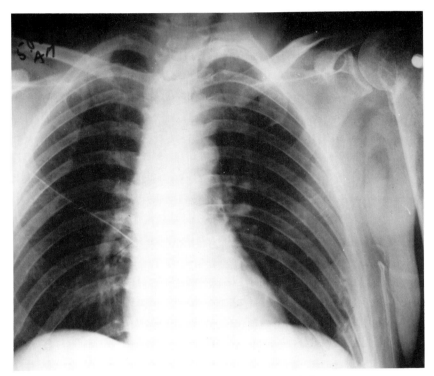

Figure 5   The Unknown Male

ANSWER

The heart is normal in size and shape. The lungs are well aerated. The aortic arch and pulmonary vessels are normal insofar as they can be seen.

There is an old fracture of the left humerus with a residual varus deformity. But, in addition, there are fractures of the left 8th through 11th ribs in the axillary line, with some callus formation about them. (The wire across the chest is a cardiac monitor lead. The faint density over the left arm is a blood pressure cuff.)

When the patient became more alert it was determined that he had a known seizure disorder which had been worked up in the past. He was also a binge drinker and often had seizures precipitated by drinking.

The rib fractures presumably were incurred during a previous binge. The house staff were, of course, correct to consider a myocardial infarction in a man who had collapsed in the street and was complaining of chest pain.

CASES 6 AND 7   TWO PATIENTS WITH TEARING CHEST PAIN

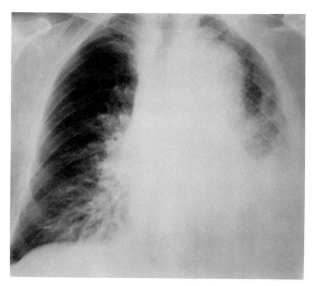

Figure 6   A   Percy Plethora

Both of these men are brought to the Emergency Room complaining of "sudden, crushing, tearing" chest pain radiating to the back. Both are in their 60's and hypertensive. One, **Mr. Percy Plethora** (Fig. 6A), is known to have an aneurysm of his aorta. The other, **Mr. Frank Fuller** (Fig. 7A), has no history of cardiac disease, but has what his family calls chronic bronchitis.

On examination, both are anxious, diaphoretic, hypertensive, and dyspneic but not in shock. Both have left ventricular hypertrophy on EKG but no evidence of myocardial infarction. Mr. Plethora has dullness and decreased breath sounds on the left. Mr. Fuller's lungs are clear to auscultation.

What are your diagnoses? How would you confirm them? How would you treat these patients? What complications must you look for?

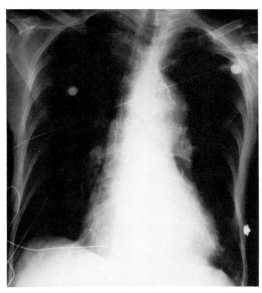

Figure 7   A   Frank Fuller

ANSWER

Mr. Plethora has a leaking aortic aneurysm. Mr. Fuller has a dissecting aortic aneurysm, but without a leak into the pleural space. Fortunately you locate old films on these patients, and the diagnoses become even more clear when you review the patients' previous chest x-rays (Figs. 6B and 7B).

In Mr. Plethora's case the widening aorta noted on the old film is no longer seen in sharp profile. The aortic margin is blurred and there is fluid (blood) in the left pleural space.

In **Mr. Fuller's** case the distance between the calcified intima and the aortic margin has increased when compared to the previous film. That distance should normally be no more than a couple of millimeters.

Now as to confirming the diagnosis, both sets of films are diagnostic in this clinical situation. However, you could tap the chest to show that the fluid is frank blood or you could do an emergency aortogram if the patient is stable. Depending on the clinical situation and the availability of a good surgical team, you might then decide to operate or to treat medically by lowering the blood pressure.

In the first case, with the leaking aneurysm, emergency surgery was necessary. In the second, medical treatment was successful.

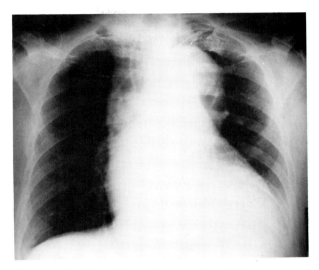

Figure 6   B   Percy's previous film

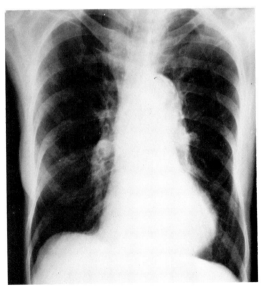

Figure 7   B   Frank's previous film

Consider the potential complications of a dissecting aneurysm. The dissection may involve and obstruct the brachiocephalic vessels and cause a stroke. The dissection may extend into the pericardium, resulting in fatal tamponade. It may involve the aortic valve and cause sudden aortic insufficiency. Or it may dissect down into the abdomen to occlude the renal arteries. Here is another patient (Fig. 7C). Which complication has occurred?

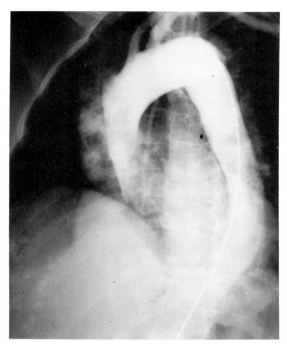

Figure 7 C   An aortic dissection with complications

ANSWER

The innominate artery does not fill with contrast. The dissection has occluded its origin. Therefore there is no blood supply to the right arm and the right carotid and vertebral arteries. The patient has suffered a stroke.

CASE 8   DULL CHEST PAIN

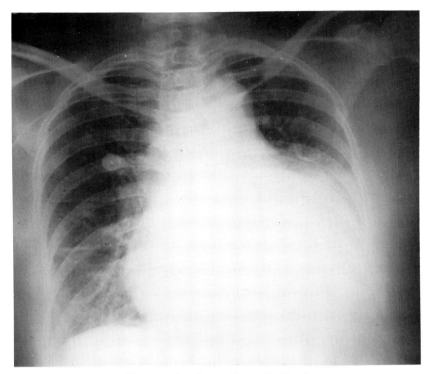

Figure 8   A   Rosalie Huff

Rosalie Huff, an obese 42-year-old mother of two, was in good health until one week ago when she developed what she thought was a cold with a low-grade fever and generalized myalgias. In the past 48 hours she has developed continuous substernal chest pain which has varied from a mild ache to a severe crushing pain. The pain radiates to her left shoulder and is somewhat relieved by sitting up and leaning forward. Her vital signs are temperature 100.6° (pr), pulse 70, blood pressure 118/68, and respiration 24 and shallow. Physical examination reveals decreased heart sounds, increased cardiac size on percussion, no clear apical impulse, a regular rhythm, and distended neck veins. This is her portable chest x-ray. Have you a diagnosis?

ANSWER

The chest film shows a large globular heart extending to the left chest wall. Allowing for portable technique, the pulmonary vessels are normal. There is no evidence of pulmonary edema. There is no double density of an enlarged left atrium at the right cardiac border. The differential is between a large heart or a pericardial effusion. How will you make this distinction?

ANSWER

There are several possible methods, including fluoroscopy, injection of carbon dioxide, an isotope scan, or an ultrasound examination. Usually the easiest first step is cardiac fluoroscopy. Under the fluoroscope the radiologist should be able to observe diminished cardiac pulsations. However, in an effusion there may be a few additional clues that there is a normally pulsating heart within the bag of pericardial fluid: the aortic pulsations may be strong and vigorous; the transmitted ventricular pulsations may be seen in the region of the left atrium where the pericardial space is only a potential space because the pericardium is "tacked down" by the pulmonary veins; or, if you are lucky, it may be possible to see a thin crescent of radiolucent epicardial fat beating away within the motionless cardiac silhouette of uniform fluid density.

In a CO_2 study, carbon dioxide injected into an antecubital vein, with the patient lying on his *left* side, will fill the right atrium and show the distance between the atrium and the cardiac margin to be increased more than the normal 3 or 4 millimeters.

An isotope scan with different radionuclides in the blood pool and the lung may show an increased space between the cardiac chambers and the lung.

All of the above methods have been and are being used. The simplest and most accurate method nowadays is probably an ultrasound scan of the heart. With the patient lying quietly on a stretcher, an ultrasound probe is passed across the chest. The "radar" image is projected onto an oscilloscope. Figure 8B is a photograph of a positive scan showing an abnormal space (the effusion) between the chest wall and the right ventricular wall, and between the left atrial wall and the lung.

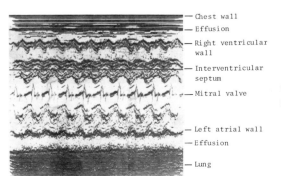

— Chest wall
— Effusion
— Right ventricular wall
— Interventricular septum
— Mitral valve
— Left atrial wall
— Effusion
— Lung

Figure 8 B   An abnormal ultrasound study showing anterior and posterior pericardial effusion

CASE 9   STEERING WHEEL INJURY AND CHEST PAIN

Alexander Eastwood Brown, a 24-year-old medical student, is brought to your Emergency Room by a police ambulance following a head-on collision in his sports car. He was wearing a seat belt but no shoulder harness and was thrown against the steering wheel. He is now complaining of severe anterior chest pain and has told the Emergency Room clerk that his admission diagnosis is "traumatic dissection of the thoracic aorta."

Except for a tachycardia and tachypnea, his vital signs are normal. His cardiorespiratory exam is also normal, but his anterior chest is extremely tender. You inform him that he probably has a chest wall injury rather than an aortic injury and send him for a chest x-ray. Here it is.

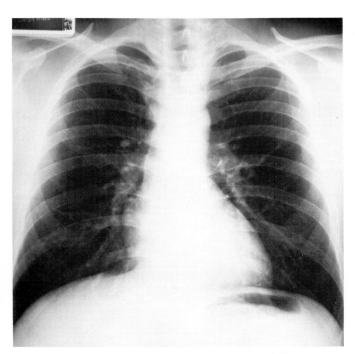

Figure 9 A   Alexander Eastwood Brown

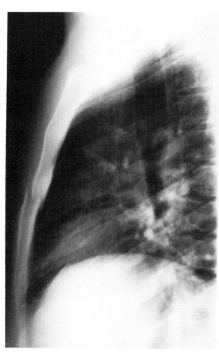

Figure 9 B

ANSWER

The PA film (Fig. 9A) is normal in appearance. There is no evidence of pneumothorax, mediastinal emphysema, or mediastinal hemorrhage. However, the lateral film of the sternum (Fig. 9B) shows that there is a depressed fracture of the sternum. There is no evidence of the commonly associated bony injuries: fractures of the clavicle or dorsal spine. Nevertheless, you decide to admit Alex for 24 hours of observation, since lacerations of the aorta or other great vessels may initially be contained by the adventitia of the vessels or adjacent soft tissue planes, only to rupture later.

SECTION II

Shortness of Breath

Dyspnea is a notoriously subjective symptom. A man held under water against his will may become short of breath in a few seconds. The same man having an argument with his wife may shout nonstop for a minute without taking a breath. On the other hand, sedentary individuals or the chronically ill may not exert themselves or may be accustomed to illness, and may not notice the gradual onset of respiratory disability. An athlete or manual laborer may notice the same disability very quickly. Some shortness of breath is psychological. We are all familiar with the anxious patient or the patient in pain who hyperventilates until he develops carpopedal spasm.

There seem to be several different mechanisms, possibly operating together, which produce the *sensation* of dyspnea. They include anoxia, hypercapnia, decreased compliance in the lung, restriction of chest wall motion, and increased work of breathing.

Therefore, it helps the radiologist enormously if the referring physician can elaborate on the symptoms of dyspnea: "dyspnea on exertion," "nocturnal dyspnea," "sudden shortness of breath," "chronic shortness of breath," "pain and shortness of breath." These symptom complexes suggest different diagnoses and direct attention to the lungs, heart, trachea or pleura, etc.

CASE 10   ACUTE DYSPNEA

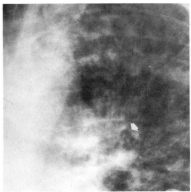

Figure 10   B

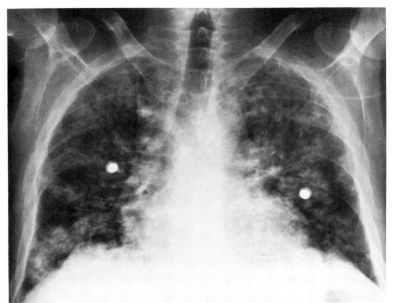

Figure 10   A   Wildcat McCoy

Bill "Wildcat" McCoy is a 47-year-old oilman who was treated at your hospital a year and a half ago for a myocardial infarction complicated by tachyrhythmias and transient congestive heart failure. He has been doing well since, but in the past few weeks he has developed progressive nocturnal wheezing and dyspnea. This afternoon he attended a prolonged business luncheon even though he felt tired, and this evening he has become acutely short of breath. This has happened in the past but usually cleared if he got up and walked over to an open window. He is now short of breath at rest and feels a "pressure" in his chest. He is visibly short of breath, diaphoretic, and slightly cyanotic. His blood pressure is 144/94, pulse 100 and regular, and respiration 34 and labored. His neck veins fill at 30 degrees elevation and his ankles are swollen. Listening to his chest, you hear moist bubbly rales and wheezes throughout. There is a ventricular gallop, but the heart sounds are strong. His EKG shows an old anterolateral myocardial infarction but no change since his last admission. This is his chest film (Fig. 10).

ANSWER

This is a portable film but the heart is grossly normal in size and shape. The lungs are abnormal. The normally sharp vascular margins, and even the cardiac margin in places, are now indistinct. This is because fluid (in this case pulmonary edema fluid) is filling up the alveoli adjacent to those structures resulting in a loss of the normally sharp air-tissue interfaces. Any sort of fluid, blood, pus, or serous transudate may produce this appearance. With this history the findings are certainly due to pulmonary edema.

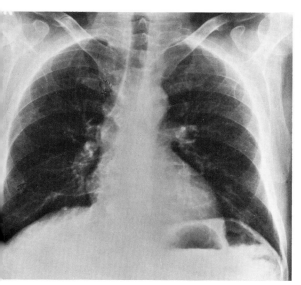

Figure 1 A   Eldridge Drudge— normal chest

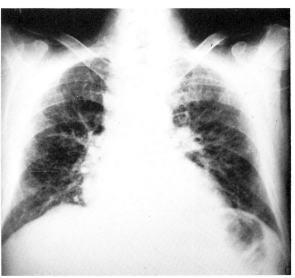

Figure 2 A   Arthur Pulling— intersitial pulmonary edema

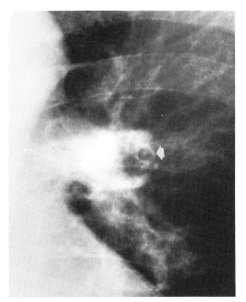

Figure 1 B   Blowup of left hilus showing normal thin wall of bronchus

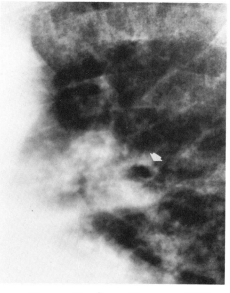

Figure 2 C   Blowup of hilus showing edema fluid around vessels and bronchus

Now look at Figures 1A and B and 2A and C. Patients Drudge and Pulling of Cases 1 and 2 and Mr. McCoy are, in fact, the same man, progressing from a normal film to interstitial edema and finally to florid pulmonary edema.

The progression of events resulting in these radiographic changes is as follows. First, the left ventricle fails to pump all the blood returned to it; this results in a rise in the end-diastolic left ventricular pressure and a consequent rise in the left atrial pressure. This is followed by an elevation of the pressure in the pulmonary veins, and, when the colloid osmotic pressure of the veins is overcome, a transudate of fluid into the interstitial or supporting tissues around the blood vessels and adjacent bronchi (see arrow).

Either the fluid in the interstitium or unexplained vascular reflexes cause vasoconstriction of the lower lobe vessels and a shunting of blood toward the upper lobes. At this point the radiologic appearance is of (1) faint blurring of the vascular outlines; (2) enlarged pulmonary vessels, especially veins, in the upper lobes; and (3) a slight increase in the amount of fluid visible around the bronchi (see arrows) and in the peripheral lymphatics (Kerley B lines) or in the pulmonary fissures (Figs. 1B, 2B, and 2C).

As the fluid continues to accumulate, the ability of the pulmonary lymphatics and thoracic duct to carry it off is exceeded. This causes fluid to accumulate in the air spaces around the vessels, first near the hila but ultimately throughout the lung (Fig. 10). As recovery occurs this whole process is reversed.

CASE 11 RIB FRACTURES AND SHORTNESS OF BREATH

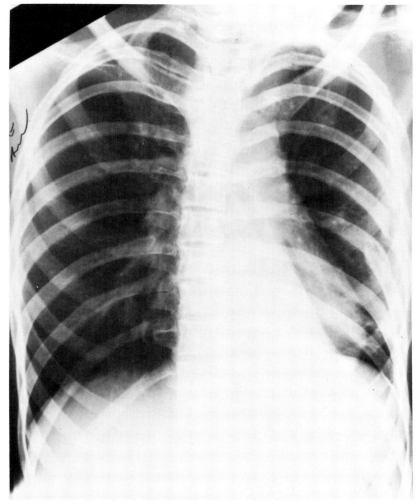

Figure 11 A   Dorothy's chest film

Dorothy Dangle is a 14-year-old girl brought to the Emergency Room four hours after falling from a tree. She has left chest pain and says she is short of breath. She has not coughed up any blood and says she is not dyspneic when she is resting quietly. Her temperature is normal as is her blood pressure, but her pulse is 80 and her respirations are shallow and rapid with a rate of 24 per minute. She is obviously splinting her left chest and the left chest wall is extremely tender. There is no crepitus in the neck. The lungs are clear to auscultation and the breath sounds are equally well heard over both apices. Her cardiac examination is normal. This is her chest film (Fig. 11A).

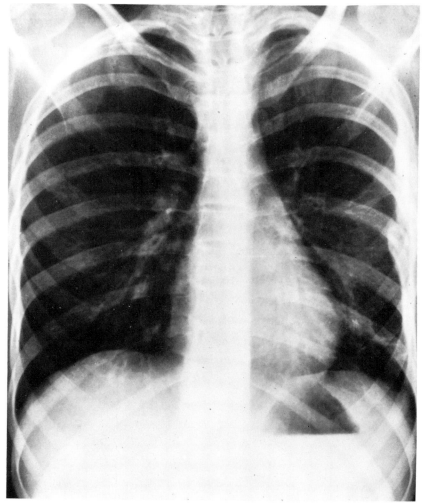

Figure 11 B   Dorothy's second film

ANSWER

There are rib fractures on the left, but there is no pneumothorax, no telltale straight line of a hydropneumothorax, and no pleural effusion. There is, however, a triangular density seen through the heart which obscures the medial portion of the slightly elevated left hemidiaphragm. The left main pulmonary artery is barely visible. These are the signs of left lower lobe collapse.

Dorothy's physical examination was essentially normal except for the rib fractures. In some cases the examiner may be able to detect a shift of the trachea toward the side of collapse and decreased tactile fremitus at the base. Wheezes may be heard if the collapse is not complete. There may be respiratory distress and even cyanosis, since the collapsed lobe is perfused but is not ventilated. This means that there is a large physiologic arteriovenous shunt.

In this instance the cause of the collapse was probably a mucus plug, since the lobe re-aerated spontaneously following pulmonary toilet (Fig. 11B). In small children or in the debilitated patient, a foreign body should be considered. In adults, especially smokers, an endobronchial carcinoma must be suspected as a cause of unexplained lobar collapse.

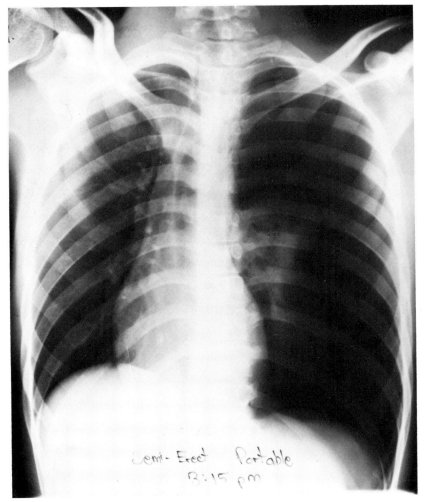

Semi- Erect   Portable
8:15 pm

Figure 12   A   Arturo Rossi

Arturo Rossi, an agitated, dyspneic 19-year-old young man, is brought to the Emergency Room by his friends. He says that he was well this morning but developed progressive shortness of breath during the afternoon. He has slight pleuritic chest pain but has not coughed up any blood. His blood pressure is 124/82 and his pulse is 84. Respirations are difficult to gauge because of his constant complaints of shortness of breath. Cursory auscultation of his chest is normal. His friends say he is excitable and that he has just broken up with his girlfriend. You suspect he might be hysterical and hyperventilating, but he is so difficult to examine that you can't be sure. Here is his portable chest film (Fig. 12A). What do you make of it? Does he need treatment?

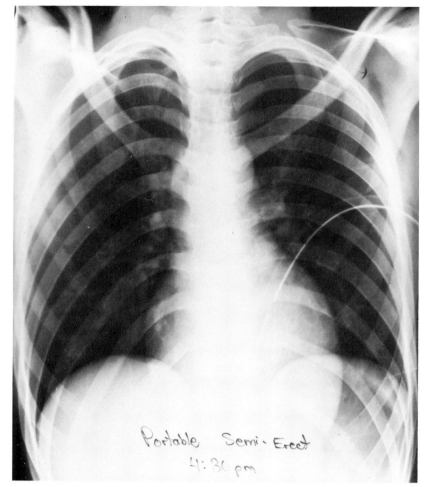

Portable Semi-Erect
4:30 pm

Figure 12 B   Rossi's film after a chest tube was inserted

ANSWER

This is a large pneumothorax. The left lung has collapsed. The mediastinum has shifted to the right and the left hemidiaphragm is depressed. This is a *tension* pneumothorax, a real medical emergency, since the expanding pneumothorax can compress the remaining aerated lung.

This pneumothorax *should* have been diagnosed on physical examination by decreased breath sounds on the left and a shift of the trachea to the right, increasing on expiration. It requires immediate treatment. In an acute emergency, if the patient is in severe respiratory difficulty, you could insert a large-bore needle through the chest wall. In this instance a chest tube was inserted and the pneumothorax re-expanded. Arturo recovered uneventfully (Fig. 12B).

Spontaneous pneumothoraces are thought to be due to ruptured subpleural blebs in the visceral pleura. They normally seal off when the lung collapses to a smaller volume. Tension pneumothoraces probably result from a rupture in the visceral pleura which acts as a one-way check valve, allowing air into the pleural space but not out.

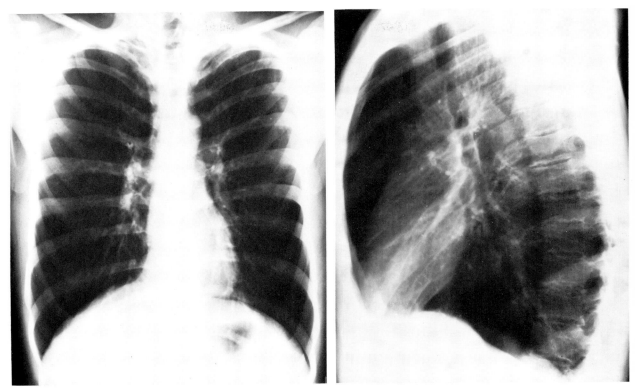

Figure 13   A and B   Henry Rush

This 22-year-old college student comes to the Emergency Room complaining of an "attack of asthma" not responding to tablets prescribed by his family doctor in Michigan. He wants "a shot of adrenalin."

Henry Rush is an anxious young man, wheezing audibly. He says he has been wheezing spasmodically since earlier in the afternoon. He has had a sore throat since this morning. He is afebrile, with respiration 24, pulse 76, and blood pressure 110/72. He sits on the edge of the examining table, leaning his arms on his knees with his shoulders hunched up. When he speaks, he telegraphs his sentences.

You hear loud wheezes and some rhonchi, but no rales. His chest is hyperresonant. Inspection of his oropharynx shows it to be reddened, but the uvula and visualized structures are not swollen. What will you do?

ANSWER

In this instance a chest film was obtained to "rule out pneumonia" (Fig. 13). You can see the barrel-shaped thorax with the increased AP diameter and the low diaphragm which result from overinflation of the lungs, but there is no pneumonia.

Acute asthmatic attacks are often precipitated and aggravated by respiratory infections. Asthmatic patients are often difficult to examine. Hence, a chest film may be very useful. On the other hand, if a respiratory infection is present, it is more likely to be a viral URI or bronchitis (neither of which will be seen on a chest film) than pneumonia. It is probably better to break the attack, listen to the chest again, and examine the sputum than to order a chest film straight off. Consider also that many recurrent asthmatics are children in whom the cumulative radiation dose from multiple chest radiographs may be significant. We would reserve the chest films for those asthmatics who clinically have pneumonia or who do not respond to treatment for bronchospasm.

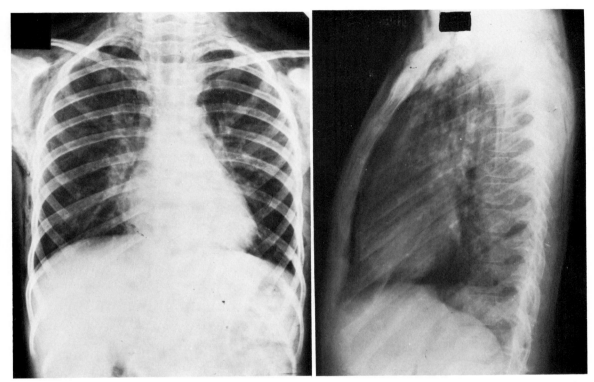

Figure 14 A   Miss Muffet

Figure 14 B   Miss Muffet

Here is another patient with asthma (Fig. 14A). **Mary Muffet** is a 5-year-old with a 2-year history of multiple asthmatic attacks which are usually treated at home. Her mother brings her to the Emergency Room at 5 A.M. because she has suddenly developed swelling in her *neck and chest wall*. She does indeed have a swelling, at the base of her neck especially, which crackles when palpated. What do you make of the chest film and how will you treat her?

ANSWER

The multiple radiolucent lines (Fig. 14A and B) seen in the soft tissues of the chest wall and neck on the PA and in the mediastinum on the lateral (look behind the sternum) are caused by air which has dissected throughout the soft tissues — subcutaneous emphysema. We think that this results from the rupture of an alveolus adjacent to a bronchus, with subsequent dissection of air back along the bronchus to the hilus of the lung and then through the mediastinum. It is rare to see such an extensive spread from the mediastinum into the chest wall. This child must have had labored breathing and emphysema for several hours at least before her mother noticed the problem. Usually the air is limited to the medias-tinum. The important thing to realize about mediastinal emphysema in the asthmatic is that it is not accompanied by pneumothorax and rarely if ever causes one. Therefore there is no need for a chest tube. When the asthma is treated and the bronchial airway pressure falls, the subcutaneous emphysema will resolve spontaneously.

The last two cases have been selected to show you what you *might* see in an asthmatic: overinflation, chest wall deformity in recurrent asthma, and mediastinal or subcutaneous emphysema in the last case. Remember, though, that the majority of young asthmatics recover between attacks, will show only temporary overinflation of the lung, or may even have completely normal chest x-rays *during* an attack.

CASE 15 "CROUP"?

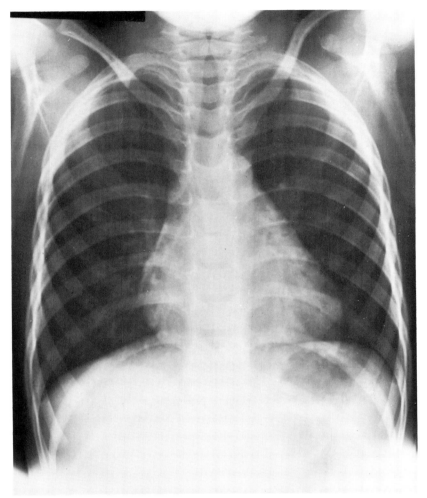

Figure 15 A   Michael O'Malley

Michael O'Malley is a 4-year-old boy brought to the Emergency Room by his mother because she thinks he has "the croup." She says that he has had a runny nose for two days. Today he has developed a cough accompanied by an inspiratory crowing sound. He doesn't have a fever, but he is coughing and becomes short of breath after a coughing fit. His mother is worried since Mike's older brother needed an emergency tracheostomy for croup. Examining him, you see a child visibly short of breath but alert and not exhausted. There are wheezes throughout his chest, but the examination is otherwise normal, and you tentatively diagnose viral laryngobronchitis (croup). This is the chest x-ray which you request (Fig. 15A).

ANSWER

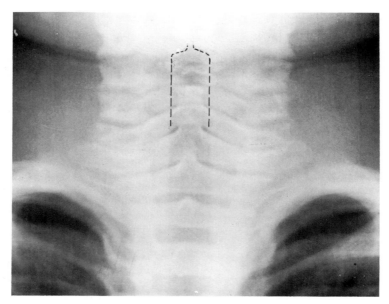

Figure 15 B   **Normal "shoulders" of subglottic space**

The lungs are overinflated (at the eleventh rib) for a sick child, but they are clear, without evidence of pneumonia. Most of the trachea looks normal, but the soft tissues beneath the vocal cords are swollen. This subglottic space is normally rectangular in shape with square "shoulders" beneath the glottis. See Figure 15B.

So, Mrs. O'Malley is right: Michael has croup. However, he is not in severe respiratory distress and he does not need a tracheostomy. Croup is a clinical diagnosis referring to a spectrum of infections involving the epiglottis, larynx, and trachea. In general they are viral infections, usually in children 3 months to 3 years of age, which can be treated conservatively with a moist air "croup tent." A fulminating bacterial infection, usually Hemophilus influenzae, may present as an acute airway obstruction, as was apparently so in the case of Mike's older brother.

CASE 16 A CHILD WITH ACUTE RESPIRATORY DISTRESS

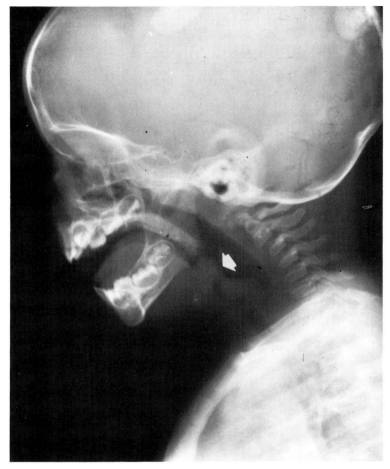

Figure 16 A   Sandy's epiglottis

Sandy Reingold is the 8-month-old daughter of a radiologist brought to your Emergency Room by her mother who says the child was well in the morning but wouldn't eat at noon, at which time her mother found her to have a temperature of 104° (pr). Initially, the child went to sleep, but in the past two hours she has developed difficulty breathing.

You see an infant in obvious respiratory distress with inspiratory stridor and supraclavicular and subcostal muscle retraction on inspiration. What is your clinical diagnosis, and how will you confirm it?

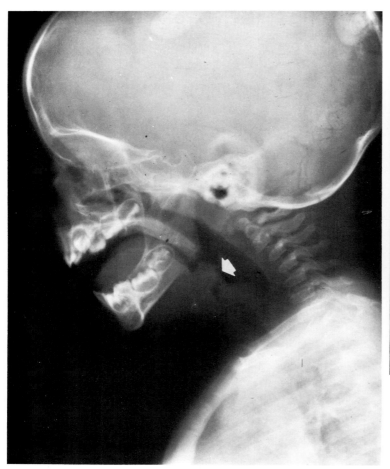

Figure 16   A   Sandy

Figure 16   B   Normal epiglott

ANSWER

Inspection of the pharynx confirms your diagnosis of epiglottitis. The pharynx is fiery red and the soft tissues are swollen. You could accept this history and the clinical findings as sufficient evidence of acute epiglottitis and initiate treatment (antibiotics, steroids, oxygen mist, and, if the distress is significant, intubation). You would not, however, struggle with the child to gain direct visualization of the epiglottis. Your manipulation and the child's screaming might increase the swelling and close off the airway. If you have any doubt as to the diagnosis you can request a *lateral* film of the neck. Figures 16A and B show a normal pharynx with a thin epiglottis (arrow), and a swollen pharynx with a swollen epiglottis (arrow).

A child like this should, of course, be accompanied by a doctor or the nurse to radiology, should be kept quiet and reassured, and should not have her head and neck manipulated for radiographic positioning. If she is severely distressed, she should be intubated rather than sent to radiology.

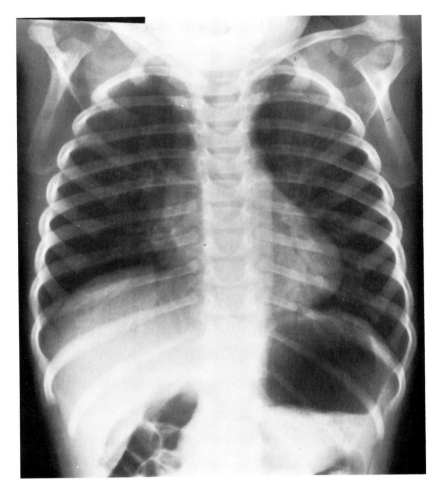

Figure 17   A   Inspiration

"Corky" Corcoran, according to his mother, is a problem child, always in trouble. This time, she says, he has swallowed a piece of a plastic soldier and has been coughing and choking since this morning. Your pediatric nurse checks his vital signs and they are normal; you examine his chest, which also seems normal, but you obtain inspiration and expiration films as a precaution. Is there an endobronchial obstruction, and, if so, where?

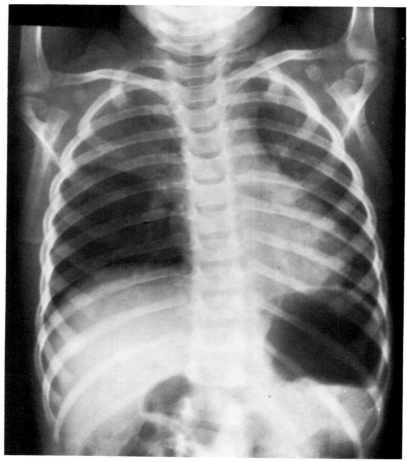

Figure 17 B   Expiration

ANSWER

Mrs. Corcoran is right. Corky has aspirated the piece of plastic and it is lodged in the right mainstem bronchus *distal* to the right upper lobe orifice. The chest looks normal on inspiration (Fig. 17A), but on expiration (Fig. 17B), when the bronchial diameters decrease, the bronchus closes around the radiolucent plastic foreign body, trapping air in the middle and lower lobes. This accounts for the relative hyperlucency of the right lower lung field on the expiration film. The foreign body was removed by bronchoscopy.

CASE 18 SUDDEN DYSPNEA AND WHEEZING IN A CHRONIC BRONCHITIC

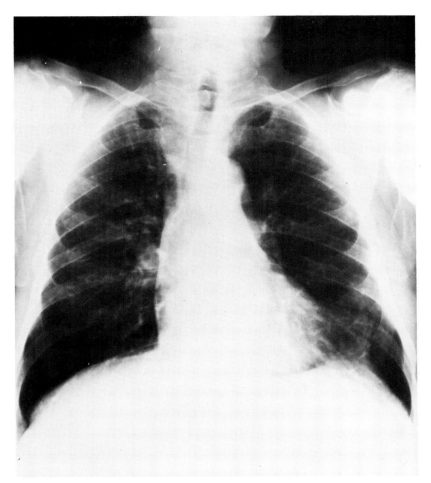

Figure 18   A   Four months ago

Mathew Turner is a 66-year-old lathe operator with a 5-year history of asthmatic bronchitis. He has been hospitalized once for a severe bronchitis, but in general he treats his "asthma" with expectorants, an inhaler, and tetracycline. Tonight he comes to the Emergency Room because of a sudden episode of dyspnea and wheezing with a heavy feeling in his chest.

His temperature is 99° (pr), pulse 90, respiration 34, and blood pressure 140/86. He is slightly cyanotic, and on auscultation you hear wheezes throughout. He has no purulent sputum. His EKG shows a right axis deviation and ST depression in leads I and II. His arterial PO_2 is 64 millimeters of mercury. Figure 18A is his chest film. How will you proceed?

ANSWER

Well, the chest film is unremarkable. The lungs are probably slightly over-inflated and there is some pleural scarring on the left. There is no evidence of pneumonia or left-sided congestive heart failure, which doesn't surprise you since there are no rales. A reasonable tentative diagnosis might be "pulmonary embolism, rule out asthmatic bronchitis with atelectasis, or pneumothorax."

What about your diagnostic approach? You know a lung scan is likely to be abnormal in a chronic bronchitic, particularly during an asthmatic attack, so you choose to proceed to a pulmonary arteriogram (Fig. 18B). How do you interpret it?

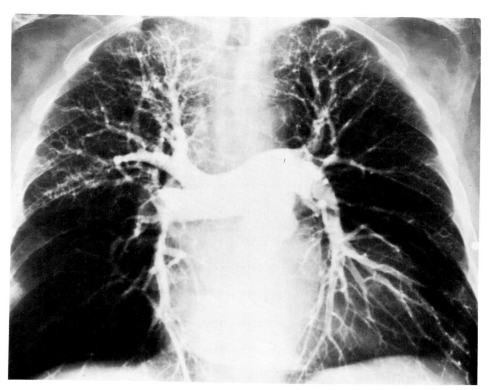

Figure 18 B   Turner's pulmonary arteriogram

ANSWER

There are clearly diminished perfusion at the right base and an abrupt cut-off to the right main pulmonary artery. There are also several long, thin filling defects (clot fragments) in the pulmonary arteries to the left lower lobe.

The abnormal pulmonary angiogram (Fig. 18B) is followed by an inferior venacavogram which shows no clots in the cava (Fig. 18C). Mr. Turner is on anticoagulants, and so far has done well. No source for the emboli was found. He has prostatism, and the pelvic veins may have been the site of origin of the clot.

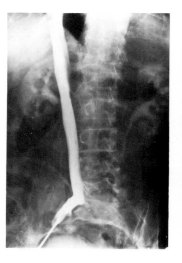

Figure 18 C   Turner's inferior venacavagram showing no clots

CASE 19   DROWNING?

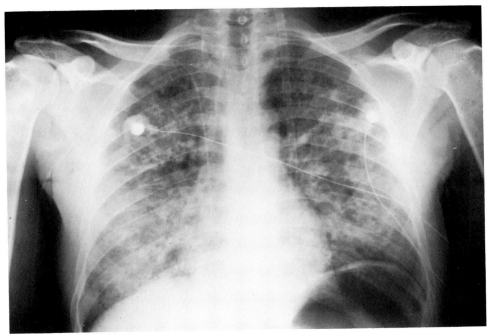

Figure 19   A   Just after arriving in the ER

This 27-year-old man was pulled unconscious from the river by a student who saw him jump from a bridge at two in the morning. The patient was breathing when rescued and is now conscious but breathing rapidly. His vital signs are normal except for tachypnea. You hear rales throughout the chest, but there is no sputum. A tracheal aspirate is bloody. A portable chest film is obtained while you continue your evaluation (Fig. 19A). What do you think of it?

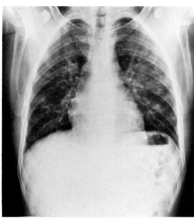

Figure 19 B Thirty-seven hours after near-drowning

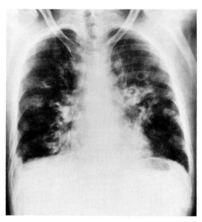

Figure 19 C and D Pulmonary abscesses from aspiration during resuscitation

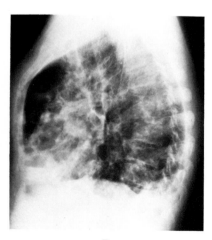

D

ANSWER

The heart is normal in size and shape. The lungs are well expanded. However, the lungs are full of some sort of fluid. You know this because the normally sharp margins of the vessels are indistinct, as are parts of the cardiac silhouette. The question is, what type of fluid is in the lungs? At first thought, you might suggest "river-water," but this is probably not the case. The lungs in near-drowning are filled with a bloody exudate. It has been thought in the past that this has been due to the effect of nonphysiologic solutions in the alveoli, and that may be true in some cases. However, there is some evidence that violent struggling for breath with a closed glottis will induce pulmonary hemorrhage and edema. The most striking radiographic feature of the lung in drowning is the very rapid clearing of the fluid. Figure 19B is a film obtained 37 hours later, showing almost complete clearing of the lungs.

Incidentally, did you notice the large amount of air in the stomach? This may be due to air swallowed while struggling for breath, or it could have been caused by attempts at resuscitation. In any case, the stomach is distended and probably also contains some swallowed water as well as normal gastric contents. If the patient aspirates, the insult to the lungs will be much worse than the drowning. Figures 19C and 19D are PA and lateral views of the chest in a man who survived a drowning two weeks before, but now has multiple pulmonary abscesses. Judging from the distribution of the abscesses anteriorly, he probably aspirated while lying on his stomach.

CASE 20 PULMONARY EDEMA IN A YOUNG MAN

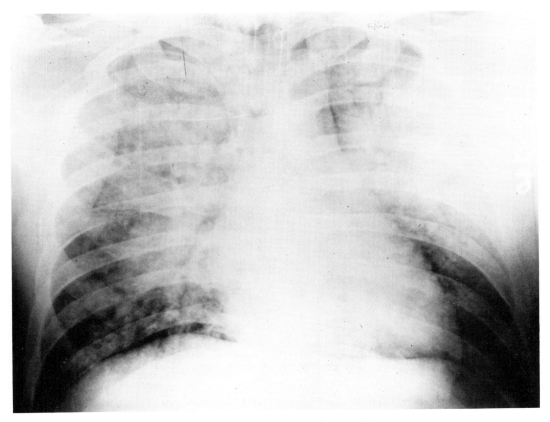

Figure 20 A   The acute film

This 28-year-old man was brought to your Emergency Room by the Fire Department Emergency Unit who responded to an anonymous call. He was found almost unconscious, gasping for breath, with pink sputum in his mouth. The rescue unit gave him oxygen on the way to the hospital.

You see a thin, disheveled man breathing rapidly and weakly. There are rales throughout his lungs and needle marks on his arms, hands, legs, and feet.

His heart sounds are good. His blood pressure is 144/86, pulse 82, and respiration rapid.

The patient is in severe respiratory distress with what sounds like pulmonary edema. You intubate him, put in a central venous line, and insert a nasogastric tube to check the gastric contents. The venous pressure is normal, the stomach empty. This is his stat portable chest film (Fig. 20A). How do you read it?

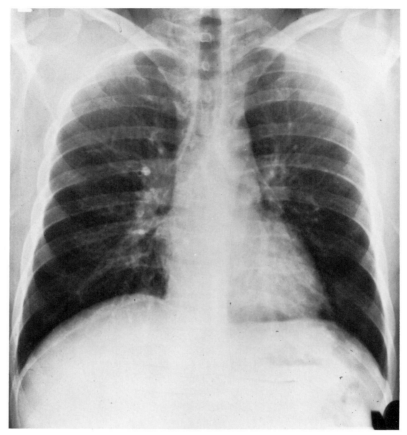

Figure 20 B   Five days later

ANSWER

This film is not much different from Case 19 (drowning). The heart is normal and the lungs are expanded, but there is a bilateral symmetrical air-space density obscuring the normal structures. As before, this is fluid in the alveoli. It could be transudate, exudate, or hemorrhage; you can't tell. However, there is a well-documented syndrome of pulmonary edema following heroin use. The edema is very much like that seen with left heart failure; in fact, some have wondered if it could be due to the cardiotoxicity of the quinine, with which the heroin is often mixed ("cut"). This has not been proved, nor has the other hypothesis that the edema results from a sudden, unusually strong dose of heroin. Since the edema, at least sometimes, follows almost instantly the "shooting up," it may be a pulmonary anaphylactic response.

At any rate, the radiograph is similar to any other kind of pulmonary edema and is nonspecific. If the patient survives, and unless there are complications such as aspiration or pneumonia, the lungs clear rapidly. The second film (Fig. 20B) was obtained five days after admission. The patient admitted that he had given himself heroin just before he collapsed.

SECTION III

Fever and Cough

CASE 21 FEVER, COUGH, AND CHEST PAIN IN A BEDRIDDEN PATIENT

Miss Effie Affable is a 64-year-old retired school teacher with angina. She has documented coronary artery disease and has had angina pectoris for several years. However, her chest pain has become much worse in the past two weeks and has even been waking her up at night. For this reason Miss Affable has been admitted to the overnight division of your Emergency Room for evaluation. Her initial physical examination is essentially normal and she has no evidence of a myocardial infarction by EKG.

However, you are called by a nurse at 2 A.M. to see her because she has a fever of 101.2°. When asked, Miss Affable says that she has pain in the right side of her chest which is worse when she coughs. She adds that she thinks she has coughed up some blood this afternoon. On physical examination there are dry rales at the bases but no other findings. The electrocardiogram is unchanged. Her temperature is elevated, as are her pulse and respiration at 78 and 25, respectively.

Here are her admission film and a second film obtained this evening. What do you make of them?

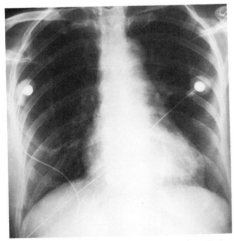

Figure 21 A Miss Affable's admission film

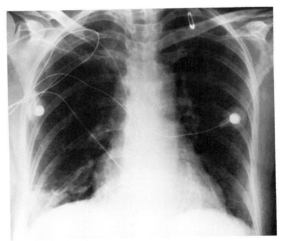

Figure 21 B Twelve hours later

ANSWER

The admission film, as noted, is a normal portable examination. Tonight's film, however, shows a roughly triangular density in the right costophrenic angle which was not present before. The chest is otherwise unchanged except for a central venous line placed in the superior vena cava shortly after admission. What is your working diagnosis and how will you proceed?

ANSWER

This could be pneumonia, but in this setting of a patient at rest with pleuritic chest pain and possible hemoptysis you should consider pulmonary embolism with pulmonary infarction as your first diagnosis. The lack of a pleural friction rub and the stable EKG are not at all uncommon in pulmonary embolism.

But how will you sustain your diagnosis? At 64, Miss Affable may already have scarring of her pulmonary capillary bed from years of smoking and occasional respiratory infections which could cause her lung scan to be abnormal even if she has not had a pulmonary embolus. On the other hand, she has severe and unstable angina. For this reason you might not want to put her through a pulmonary angiogram, which will entail several needle punctures and a catheter placed in the vena cava, if not in the heart. (You can usually inject the contrast material satisfactorily from a catheter placed in the inferior vena cava. You do not have to traverse the right atrium and ventricle with the catheter if it seems dangerous to do so.)

In this case you decide to try the scan first. If the scan shows a defect at the right base alone, it will be of no help, since pneumonia would cause the same defect as would an infarction. But, if there are other clear-cut defects in the scan, they will most likely be due to other emboli not resulting in infarction. The defects must be definite. Minor irregularities in the perfusion pattern could be due to previous lung infection. Here is the scan (Fig. 21C). What do you think?

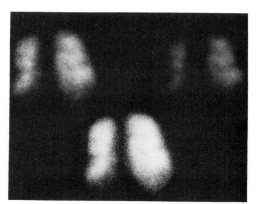

Figure 21 C The emergency lung scan (frontal view, three intensities)

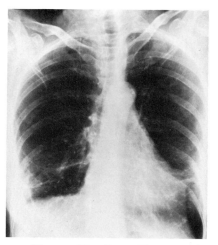

Figure 21 D Two weeks after the infarct—scarring and atelectasis at the right base

ANSWER

It is clearly an abnormal scan with multiple areas of diminished perfusion in addition to the right base.

Figure 21D shows Miss Affable's chest film two weeks later. The infarcted lung, a sterile "pneumonitis" responsible for the fever and chills, is scarring down with associated thickening of the pleura and some platelike atelectasis. This is a typical course for a pulmonary infarction. It is classic when you see it, but remember that many emboli do not result in infarction, and many go undiagnosed.

CASE 22   COUGH AND FEVER

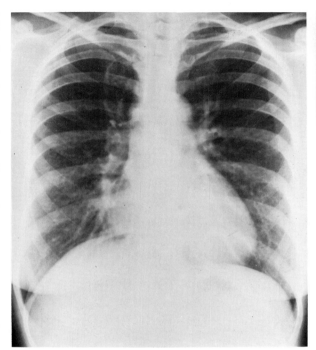
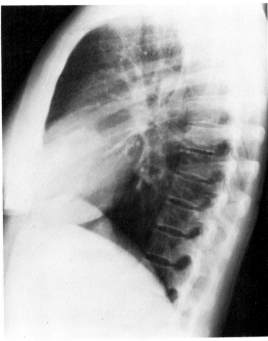

A   B

Figure 22   A and B   Patsy's chest film

Miss Patsy Jolly is a 35-year-old waitress who comes to the Emergency Room because of fever and cough. Last week she had a cold with a runny nose and a nonproductive cough. It seemed to be getting better, but the cough has persisted and in the past three days has become productive of yellow sputum. She has a fever of 101° (po) and a leukocytosis of 14,000. You hear coarse rales over the right anterior and lateral chest on physical examination. There is no dullness to percussion, and the rest of the examination is normal. You obtain some sputum and send her to X-Ray while you do a Gram stain. The sputum contains multiple encapsulated gram-positive diplococci and abundant white blood cells, confirming your diagnosis of (pneumococcal) pneumonia. Does the chest x-ray confirm the physical examination and sputum examination (Fig. 22A and B)?

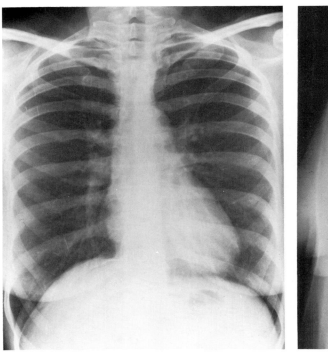

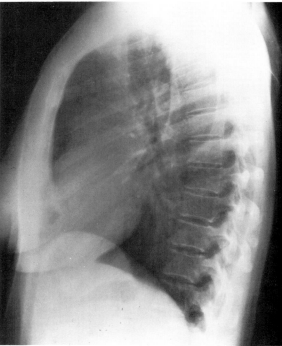

C

D

Figure 22   C and D   **Patsy's normal film**

Answer

Yes, it does. The radiographic findings are subtle, but abnormal. The right cardiac margin is indistinct on the PA view and there is an area of increased density seen through the cardiac silhouette on the lateral—a right middle lobe pneumonia.

You give Miss Jolly a prescription for oral penicillin and an appointment to return within a week, at which time she feels and looks fine. Her chest film has returned to normal (Fig. 22C and D).

This is a typical case of pneumonia following an upper respiratory infection. It is *also* a typical University Hospital workup. A great many practicing physicians would have treated this lady at home, or in an office, with a physical examination and a broad-spectrum antibiotic. They might or might not have cultured her sputum. She would have recovered just as well, and the cost of her medical care would have been much less without x-rays, CBC, and sputum culture. The abbreviated approach may occasionally lead to mistakes, but it is worth wondering what the most efficient approach would be.

CASE 23 FEVER AND NONPRODUCTIVE COUGH IN A SCHOOL GIRL

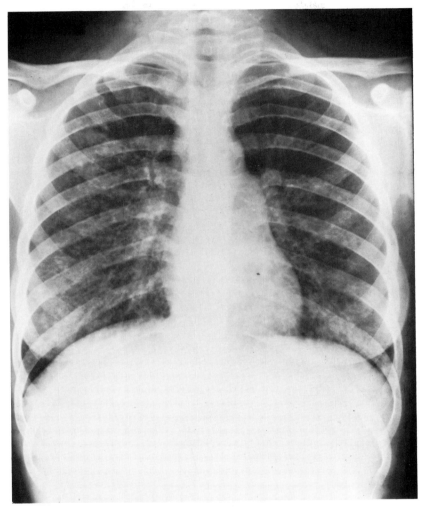

Figure 23 A   Penny's original film

Penny Bright, a 14-year-old school girl, is brought to the Emergency Room by her parents because of a four-day history of fever and dry cough. She has a temperature of 100.4° (po), but she does not look seriously ill. On auscultation, you hear coarse rales throughout both lungs.

The remainder of her examination is normal. She is unable to produce any sputum. Her white count is 5,400 with a normal differential. Penny says she has a "virus" and that "a lot of the kids at school do too." Her parents "worry too much." Figure 23A is her chest film.

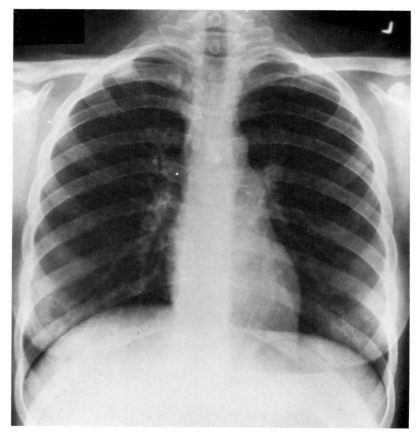

Figure 23　B　Two weeks later

ANSWER

Well, this is a fairly striking film for a relatively asymptomatic child. There is a diffuse increase in the reticular pattern of the lungs, normally produced by branching pulmonary vessels. There are abnormal densities here, produced by multiple areas of pneumonia in a peribronchial or interstitial distribution throughout the lung. The bronchi and lymphatics run with the arteries, and the peribronchial densities therefore look much like perivascular densities, as you would expect. In this instance (proved by complement titers), we are dealing with a Mycoplasma infection which has spread down the airway into the bronchi and surrounding supportive structures. This is a fairly common pattern for viral and Mycoplasma pneumonias in adults, though this infection is more widespread throughout the lungs than is usually seen.

Penny finally coughed up a little sputum which contained a few mononuclear cells. She was sent home with instructions to return for a followup visit in a week (or sooner if she felt worse or developed purulent sputum). On culture, her sputum produced only "normal throat flora." Two weeks later her chest film was normal (Fig. 23B).

CASE 24 A MAN WITH RUSTY SPUTUM

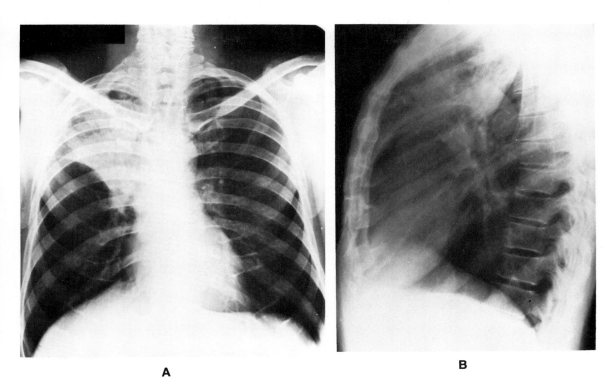

A   B

Figure 24   A and B   Mr. Friendly's chest films

Mr. Bill Friendly is a 55-year-old TV repairman who has had "a bad cold" for a week but came to the Emergency Room tonight because he has coughed up some rusty sputum. You elicit the additional history that he has smoked heavily since the age of 14 and has had a morning cough for years. The cough has been worse than usual for about three months.

He is febrile, with a temperature of 101° (po), pulse 80, respiration 22 at rest, and blood pressure 124/84. He looks ill. You hear wheezes and rales on the right, especially over the apex and anteriorly. There is diminished tactile fremitus over the right upper lobe compared to the left. You're not sure about dullness. What does the chest film show, and what is your tentative diagnosis?

ANSWER

In Figures 24A and B there is consolidation of the right upper lobe visible on both PA and lateral views, and there is some collapse or atelectasis of the lobe, since the minor fissure is elevated. But you suspected this, since you heard wheezing on the right.

Clearly a lobar pneumonia alone *could* produce this clinical and radiographic appearance, but with loss of volume in the lobe and the wheezing you must consider a likely cause of the bronchial narrowing: bronchogenic carcinoma. Mr. Friendly wanted to return home but was persuaded to come into the hospital. He did have a pneumococcal pneumonia, but sputum cytologic studies were positive. He was found to have squamous cell carcinoma in the right main bronchus with spread to the hilar nodes (we can probably see them on the PA film). Unfortunately, he died at surgery.

Pneumonia that is associated with significant atelectasis should alert you to the possibility of an endobronchial lesion (in children a foreign body and in adults a tumor).

CASE 25 A LADY WITH FEVER, CHILLS, AND PURULENT SPUTUM

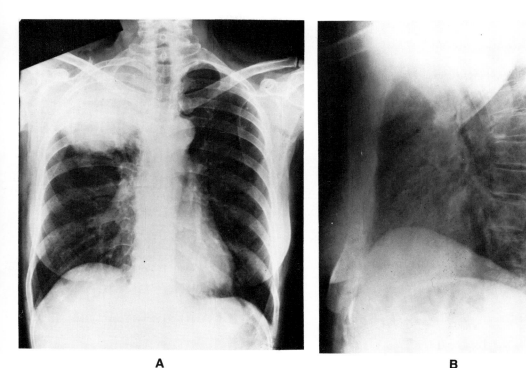

Figure 25   A and B   Mrs. Gray's chest films

Mrs. Ernestine Gray, a 58-year-old widow, comes to the Emergency Room because of fever and cough. She thinks she has pneumonia. Mrs. Gray has been in good health most of her life, but she developed diabetes last year and was recently treated for a urinary tract infection. She has had fever and cough for the past four days and pain in the right shoulder since yesterday.

Examining her, you find: temperature 103° (po), pulse 84, respiration 25, and blood pressure 140/88. She looks ill. There are rales in the right upper chest with decreased breath sounds and dullness to percussion. Manipulation and palpation of her shoulder does not worsen her chest pain, but coughing does. Her sputum is thick and green. These are her chest films (Fig. 25A and B). What is her problem?

ANSWER

There is a dense consolidation or mass in the right upper chest. Is it a mass or consolidation? Clinically it is a pneumonia. On the PA film it is a little difficult to be sure, but on the lateral the density clearly stops at the major fissure, which is bowed slightly backward. This *segmental* distribution is more typical of pneumonia than tumor. Moreover, the backward bowing of the fissure (for reasons we fail to understand) is often seen in Klebsiella pneumonia, a pneumonia more common in debilitated individuals, alcoholics, diabetics, and patients previously treated with broad-spectrum antibiotics. The sputum smear showed many gram-negative rods. Both sputum and blood cultures grew out Klebsiella.

SECTION IV

Hemoptysis

Cancer and tuberculosis have been the feared causes of hemoptysis. TB is much less common than it was, but bronchogenic carcinoma is on the increase. Other relatively common causes of hemoptysis are chronic bronchitis, bronchiectasis, pneumonia, pulmonary embolism, and mitral stenosis. Most of these conditions are associated with clearly abnormal x-rays. However, the chest film may be normal in bronchitis, bronchiectasis, pulmonary embolism, and occasionally in carcinoma. This may cause you and the radiologist a good deal of anxiety. How would you "workup" a middle-aged patient who comes to the emergency room with recurrent hemoptysis and a normal chest film?

The bloody sputum should be examined and cultured for evidence of bacterial or fungal infection. Sputum should be sent for cytologic examination for malignant cells. A skin test for tuberculosis should be obtained, since a conversion from a negative to a positive skin test might be the only clue of tuberculosis. Most of us would follow these steps with bronchoscopy and bronchial washings or with bronchial brushing. A bronchogram might reveal the presence of a tumor or bronchiectasis, which is invisible on a plain film of the chest.

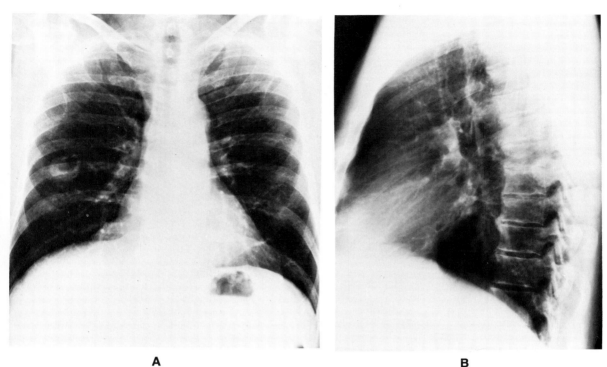

A

B

Figure 26   A and B   Mr. Tredd's chest films

Mr. Peter Tredd is a 63-year-old mailman who has been in excellent health all his life. He smokes and has a smoker's cough, to which he has paid no attention, but this Sunday evening he coughed up some bright red blood. He is worried and comes to you in the Emergency Room because his family doctor is on vacation.

Mr. Tredd's physical examination is completely normal. He cannot raise any sputum or blood now. Here are his chest PA and lateral (Fig. 26A and B). What do you make of them?

ANSWER

There is a cavitating lesion in the right lower lobe, clearly seen on the PA and visible over the spine on the lateral. The rest of the chest is normal. Do you think this is an abscess or a tumor, and how will you tell?

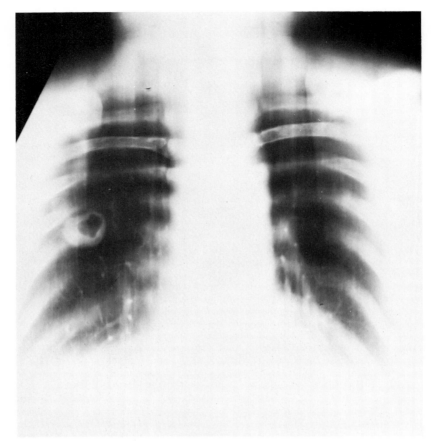

Figure 26 C   Tomographic cut of Tredd's nodule

ANSWER

First you have to see the lesion clearly. On the PA view it looks like a round lesion with an irregular thick-walled cavity, more likely to be cancer than a less well-defined thin-walled cavity. You could get coned spot films of the lesion at fluoroscopy, and at the same time examine the hila for evidence of hilar and subcarinal adenopathy. Tomography of the chest will give much of the same information. Both were performed in this case. The tomogram (Fig. 26C) delineates the lesion clearly. It proved to be a squamous carcinoma of the lung. Mr. Tredd is doing well one year after a lobectomy.

Most "coin lesions," even if cancer, do not cause hemoptysis or other symptoms. This one, however, has an air-filled cavity which must communicate with a bronchus, so it is not surprising that the patient coughed up blood.

CASE 27 HEMOPTYSIS, CHEST PAIN, AND COLLAPSE

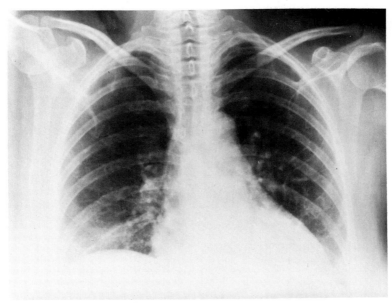

**Figure 27 A   Mrs. Doolittle's portable chest film
(ignore obscuring of lung bases by breast shadows)**

Mrs. Barbara Doolittle, a 46-year-old housewife, is brought to the Emergency Room by ambulance, having collapsed in the bathroom of her home. She has severe right pleuritic chest pain and has coughed up a small amount of blood. Except for slight tachycardia and tachypnea, her vital signs are normal. Her lungs are normal on examination. She has no calf tenderness, but as you examine her she gives a history of phlebitis in the right thigh and tells you that she has been taking Coumadin for three months. This is her chest film. Do you think she has a pulmonary embolus?

ANSWER

The chest film is normal, but don't let that dissuade you from your diagnosis: a normal chest film is the most common radiologic presentation of pulmonary embolism. Now the question is, how do you confirm the diagnosis: a scan or an angiogram?

Either scan or pulmonary angiogram would be useful if strongly positive, but if there is any doubt, you are going to need the angiogram. Mrs. Doolittle is already on anticoagulants and has a source for emboli. If she has emboli it will be necessary to ligate her inferior vena cava. In a situation like this we would utilize the angiogram which would be definitive. Here it is (Fig. 27B). What do you think?

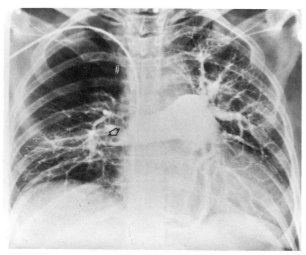

Figure 27 B   Mrs. Doolittle's pulmonary angiogram

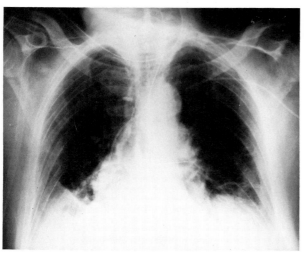

Figure 27 C   The surgical patient's abnormal chest film

Figure 27   D   His grossly abnormal lung scan (frontal view)

ANSWER

The catheter has been advanced from the antecubital vein through the superior vena cava, right atrium, and right ventricle to the pulmonary outflow tract. Clearly the angiogram is abnormal. There is a lobulated filling defect in the right main pulmonary artery blocking most of the blood flow to the right lung (arrow). In some centers a clot this large would be removed surgically, particularly if the patient were severely anoxic. In this case a caval ligation was performed and Mrs. Doolittle recovered.

The preceding cases of pulmonary embolism with or without infarction have been chosen because of their "classic" histories and films. But, in a sense, they could be misleading. Probably less than 25% of all *diagnosed* pulmonary emboli have the triad of dyspnea, chest pain, and hemoptysis. In several studies the incidence of symptoms has been approximately as follows: dyspnea 80%, chest pain 70%, fever and rales 60%, and hemoptysis 30%.

Also, let us put in a word for the lung scan. The most useful scan is a completely normal scan. A slightly abnormal scan could be due to old emboli, infections, asthma, congestive heart failure, or anything else which would alter pulmonary perfusion. However, a scan can be useful even in the presence of a moderately abnormal chest film. Figures 27C and D are the abnormal portable chest film and lung scan of a 69-year-old surgical patient with a long history of bronchitis and congestive heart failure who became suddenly dyspneic on the third postoperative day. His scan shows almost no blood flow at all on the left; just a little perfusion is evident at the left apex. This was a pulmonary embolism.

CASE 28   A YOUNG MAN WITH FATIGUE AND HEMOPTYSIS

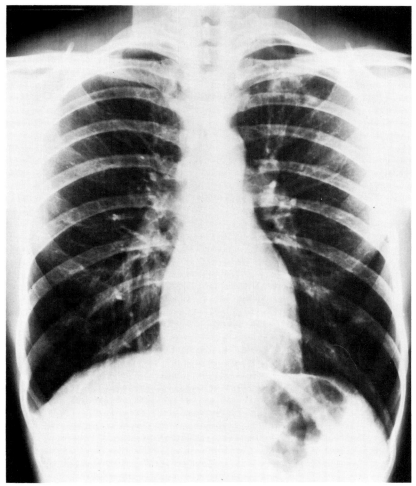

Figure 28   A   David's PA chest

David Baring is a 25-year-old garage mechanic sent to the Emergency Room by his boss because he is coughing up blood. At first David insists that he is fine, but when quizzed he admits that he has been tired for the past several weeks and that he has been coughing up blood for the past 10 days. He has a temperature of 99° (po), but his physical examination is completely normal. You are not very impressed by the story but send him for a chest film (Fig. 28A).

ANSWER

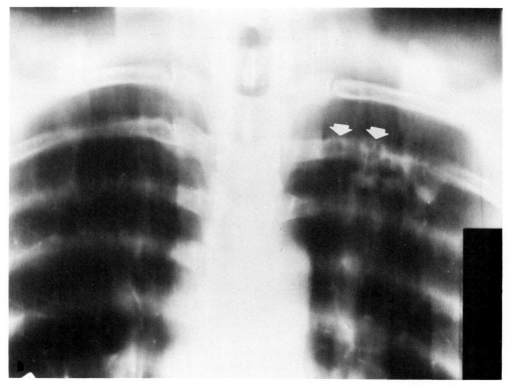

Figure 28 B   Tomographic cut through cavities in left upper lobe

Do you see those densities in the left upper lobe? Would you like to see them better? Look at the tomographic cut (Fig. 28B).

This is a cavitating pneumonia in the apical posterior segment of the left upper lobe, typical of tuberculosis. TB is still seen. This disease is more common in the poor, in Indians and Eskimos, and in alcoholics, but it is still seen in healthy young men. Acid-fast stains of a tracheal aspirate were positive.

Some TB is resistant to commonly used drugs. How soon after beginning treatment would you expect to see improvement on the radiograph? About 2 weeks to a month. Symptoms would improve sooner.

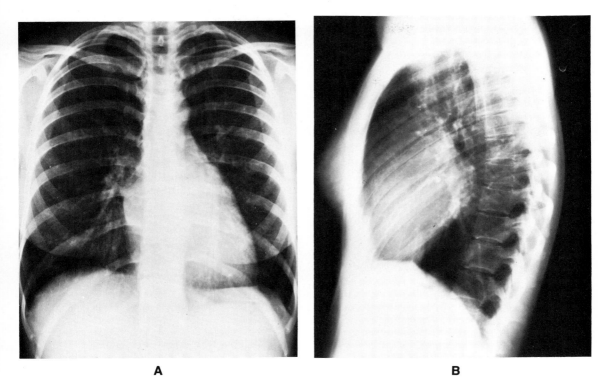

A   B

Figure 29 A and B   Amy's chest film

Amy Grady is a 24-year-old girl who comes to the Emergency Room because she has been coughing up small amounts of blood off and on for a week. She has not had fever or night sweats but has been "run down" for the past year. You are in the middle of suturing an extensive knife wound and don't want her sitting in the waiting room if she has open tuberculosis, so you send her straight to X-Ray. Here are her PA and lateral films (Fig. 29A and B). What do you think of them?

ANSWER

The heart is enlarged; more than that, its shape is abnormal. The upper left heart border is ballooned outward, and there is a double density behind the right heart border. The lateral film confirms that the left atrium is enlarged and also shows that the right ventricle is enlarged, filling up the retrosternal space. The main pulmonary arteries are slightly enlarged, as were the upper lobe vessels. These are, of course, the stigmata of mitral valve disease. Hemoptysis is encountered in about 10% of patients with mitral valve disease and may even be the presenting complaint. In this instance, Amy knew that she had a heart murmur, but she had never had medical attention, was not taking penicillin, and did not realize that her tiredness was due to her heart.

The pathogenesis of the hemoptysis is not clear. In otherwise asymptomatic mitral valve disease it is probably related to an acute rise in pulmonary venous pressure with bleeding from pulmonary veins. In decompensated mitral valve disease it may be due to rupture of the collaterals that form between the pulmonary and bronchial arteries.

CASE 30 AN ALCOHOLIC LADY WITH HEMOPTYSIS AND FEVER

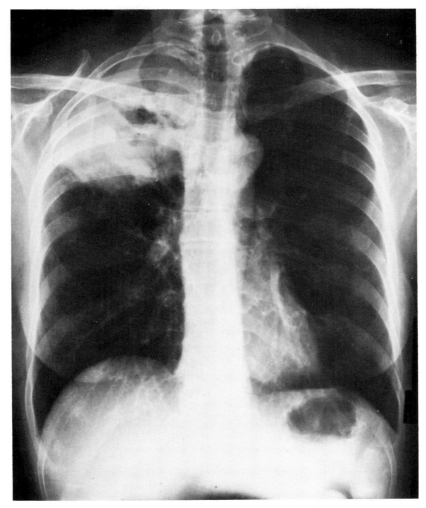

Figure 30   Mrs. Bland's chest film

Mrs. Gertrude Bland is brought to the Emergency Room by the police who were called by her landlady. She looks seriously ill and is coughing up bloody (currant-jelly) sputum. She has the odor of alcohol on her breath. Her temperature is 102° (po), but her pulse and blood pressure are normal. She is not in respiratory distress. There are rales and rhonchi at the right apex. You give a sputum sample to your intern for a Gram stain and send Mrs.

Bland to X-Ray. In the meantime you phone the landlady and get the history that Mrs. Bland is a heavy drinker, but that she is usually well dressed and, so far as the landlady knows, has never had delirium tremens.

The radiologist gives you a call to say that her chest film is abnormal and that she might have tuberculosis. Here is the film. What do you think?

ANSWER

There is a right upper lobe density with a cavity. As the radiologist goes over the film with you, he notices that the smooth inferior margin of the density seen on the PA film is due to an elevated minor fissure. That means volume loss. Could Mrs. Bland have aspirated, or could there be pneumonia behind an obstructing tumor at the hilus? Well, these are reasonable possibilities, but the sputum is full of gram-negative rods which prove to be *Klebsiella aerobacter*. Mrs. Bland is in fact the same patient as Mrs. Gray of Case 25, this time with a fictional history.

Even with treatment, this sticky necrotizing pneumonia clears very poorly and cavitates. Staphylococcus and some thickly encapsulated pneumococci may do the same thing. The bloody, currant-jelly sputum is said to be classic for Klebsiella.

SECTION V

Abdominal Pain

The differentiation of various sorts of abdominal pain can be difficult. The most useful information is the precipitating cause (food, drink, bowel movements, urination), the location of the pain, and the duration of the pain. Intensity is notoriously difficult to evaluate.

A plain film of the abdomen does not, unfortunately, often help to differentiate those vague intestinal complaints encountered so often. However, a series of films may help, and the plain film may be very useful in patients with severe or catastrophic abdominal pain. If there is associated bleeding, vomiting, or diarrhea, contrast studies may be necessary for diagnosis.

A word about the radiologic approach to the acute abdomen. It seems obvious that a careful history and close consultation between internist or surgeon and radiologist are wasted if the radiographs obtained are not of excellent quality. Modern equipment allows us to obtain really good portable chest radiographs. It does not yet permit good portable abdominal films. The patient must be brought to the Radiology Department. If he is too ill to be brought to X-Ray, he should probably be on the way to the O.R.

Carefully monitored AP and decubitus or upright films of the abdomen (usually accompanied by chest films) can encompass the range of radiographic density from bone to calcium, soft tissue, fluid, and fat, to air or some other gas. On a perfect film you should be able to see the normal fat planes of the flank, the retroperitoneal viscera, the bowel, and the fluid within it.

With good films, as little as a few cubic centimeters of air free within the peritoneum or in an abscess cavity may be seen. Obliteration of a flank "stripe" or psoas margin may indicate inflammatory edema or blood, or urine in the normal fat planes. An irregularly thickened bowel wall may indicate ulcerative or granulomatous colitis, bowel infarction, or hemorrhage. Faint calcifications may tip you off to appendicoliths, renal or gall stones, or an abdominal aneurysm. Any of these signs may be missed if the films are not of excellent quality.

CASE 31 INTERMITTENT ABDOMINAL CRAMPS IN A HEALTHY WOMAN

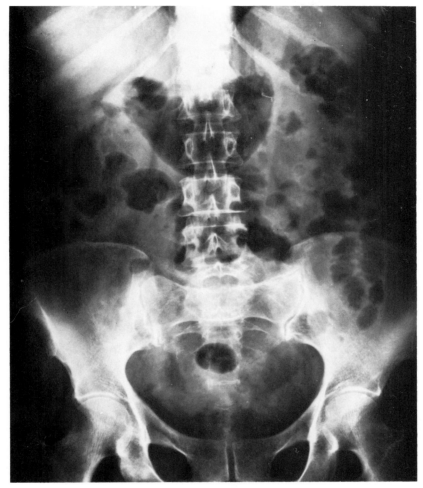

Figure 31 A   Maybelle's plain film

Mrs. Maybelle Barnstable, a 55-year-old nurse's aide, has just finished the 4 to 11 P.M. shift and comes to see you in the Emergency Room because of abdominal pain which has been getting worse all evening. She describes it as a sharp, aching pain in the midabdomen which comes in waves lasting about half an hour each time. She has felt constipated and nauseated but has had no vomiting or diarrhea. Mrs. Barnstable says she has had no previous medical or surgical illness and takes no medicines.

You find her to be a plump woman who doesn't look seriously ill. Her vital signs and examination of the chest are normal. Her bowel sounds are normal, or possibly slightly increased, with an occasional "pinging" sound. However, the abdomen is soft without guarding and there are no masses. Pelvic and rectal examinations are normal. This is the plain film of her abdomen (Fig. 31A). The chest film did not contribute any further information and is not reproduced.

ANSWER

The only thing about this film which might worry you is the amount of gas in the small bowel. The bones and retroperitoneal fat planes are normal, so far as they can be seen. That is the fundus of the stomach in the midline. (The patient is supine so the air rises to the antrum and fundus, the most anterior part of the stomach.) There is a moderate amount of gas in the upper abdomen; some, such as that over the left iliac wing, is clearly in small bowel, with closely spaced valvulae conniventes. Yet, there is no gas which can clearly be said to be in the distal large bowel or rectum. The appearance of the intestinal gas pattern is, as they say, nonspecific, but a little worrisome in this clinical setting; early ileus or obstruction could look like this. What will you do?

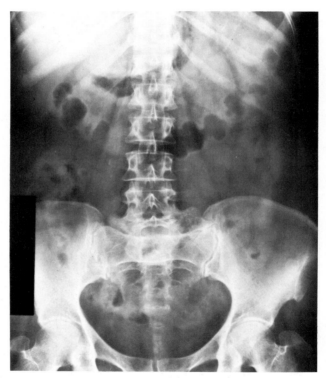

Figure 31 B   Maybelle's abdomen the next morning

ANSWER

In reality, your disposition of the case would depend upon nuances of the patient's appearance and history, on the patient's home situation, on the bed situation in your hospital, and possibly on what the patient wants. In fact, Mrs. Barnstable was admitted to the overnight ward with an order for a followup KUB in the morning. She had two episodes of diarrhea during the night, but the pain ceased. Her morning plain film (Fig. 31B) is normal. There is now less gas in the small bowel and some in the transverse colon.

This is a fairly typical case, except that usually no second film is obtained if the patient feels well. Watchful waiting and followup films are often very important in the management of abdominal pain.

CASE 32　A CHILD WITH RIGHT-SIDED ABDOMINAL PAIN

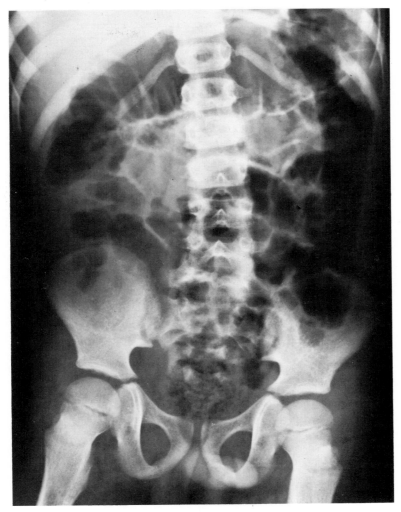

Figure 32　Napoleon Garfinkle

Napoleon Garfinkle, a 7-year-old school boy, is brought to the Emergency Room by his mother who says he has been constipated for the past 2 days, won't eat, and is now complaining of a stomach-ache. While you examine the boy you get the additional history that the pain is worsening, that it is now more on the right side, and that the child is now nauseated.

Napoleon's temperature is 100.2° (po), but his white count is normal. His bowel sounds are somewhat decreased, and there is tenderness to deep palpation in the right lower quadrant. There is no rebound tenderness, but a gentle rectal examination reveals definite tenderness on the right. Hyperextension of the right leg causes right flank pain. The chest is normal. Urinalysis is normal.

You make a tentative diagnosis of acute appendicitis and request a plain film of the abdomen. Here it is (Fig. 32). Does it confirm your diagnosis?

ANSWER

Yes, it does. That scoliosis of the lumbar spine concave to the right is caused by spasm of the psoas muscle irritated by an inflamed appendix. Although the abdomen is full of swallowed air, there is very little gas in the right lower quadrant. The gas-containing bowel is displaced by an inflammatory mass. The lower portions of the right psoas margin and flank stripe have been infiltrated with edema fluid and are no longer visible. Two further possible signs of appendicitis are missing: an air-fluid level in the cecum (local ileus), and an appendicolith (which is present in 5 to 10% of cases of acute appendicitis).

Supposing the plain film was normal? Would you have changed your diagnosis? I hope not, with all these clinical signs of appendicitis. Napoleon was taken to the O.R., and the offending appendix was removed.

CASE 33 RECURRENT PAIN AND INDIGESTION

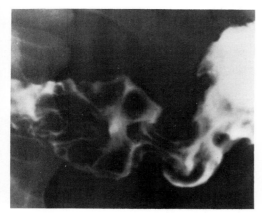

Figure 33 A   Spot film of the duodenal bulb

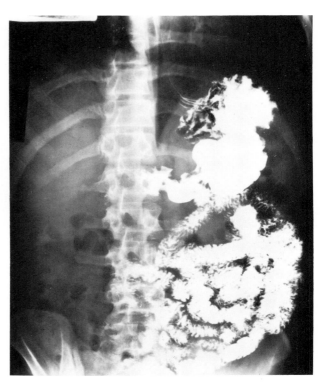

Figure 33 C   Overhead film of the stomach and proximal small bowel

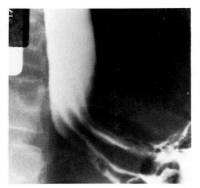

Figure 33 B   Spot film of the distal esophagus

Mr. Edward Pressing is a 47-year-old salesman with gnawing midabdominal pain. Mr. Pressing has been in good health until recently, when two things happened: he got divorced, and his father died of stomach cancer. For about a month Pressing has had episodic midabdominal pain and nausea, sometimes relieved by eating. He has lost about 5 lbs. in the last two weeks and is afraid that he too has carcinoma, so he comes to see you in the Emergency Room this Saturday night.

Edward does not look ill, and his vital signs are normal. You hand him over to your medical student, who further explores the relationship of his stomach pain to his meals: the pain is more common in the evening and at night, is often relieved by a good meal or a sandwich, but is worsened by Mr. Pressing's usual nightcap highball.

The medical student suspects that the problem is a duodenal ulcer. The CBC is normal and the stool guaiac negative, but he inserts a nasogastric tube anyway. The gastric aspirate is Töpfer-positive (i.e., acid is present) and guaiac-negative. The stomach is empty. The medical student diagnoses a probable duodenal ulcer and you agree, but Pressing is still distraught and now wants to be admitted to the hospital.

You relate this tale of woe to the radiology resident, who agrees that since the stomach is empty, he might as well confirm your diagnosis tonight instead of tomorrow morning. Here is the upper G.I. series (Fig. 33A, B, and C). Is the medical student correct?

ANSWER

Yes, Mr. Pressing does have a duodenal ulcer, an absolute classic, smack in the middle of the posterior wall of the duodenal bulb, with little folds of mucosa radiating toward the ulcer niche. The mucosal folds of the proximal duodenum are also slightly swollen by edema, but the esophagus, stomach, and proximal small bowel are normal. You inform Pressing of the diagnosis and send him home, much reassured, with diet instructions and an appointment to your clinic.

CASE 34 A BARTENDER WITH RECURRENT
MIDABDOMINAL PAIN

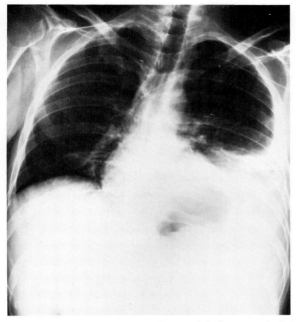

Figure 34 A Frenchie's upright chest film

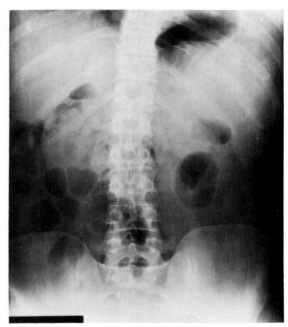

Figure 34 B Plain film of Frenchie's abdomen

Jean "Frenchie" Laroche is a 36-year-old former hockey player, now turned bartender. He comes to you complaining of severe abdominal pain that has been progressively worsening over the past 3 days. You elicit the additional history that Frenchie consumes about a quart of his own goods each evening, and that he has had intermittent abdominal pain for more than a year, usually following drinking sprees. He thinks he may have an ulcer. He has not noticed dark stools. Although the pain has made him vomit on occasion, he has not had coffee-ground or bloody vomitus.

Tonight Frenchie looks in pain but well nourished. His temperature is 99.6° (po), pulse 76, respiration 20, and blood pressure 125/75. Examination of the chest is normal except for dullness and a few coarse rales at the left base. His abdomen is more impressive, with diminished bowel sounds, guarding, and rebound tenderness in the epigastrium. His hematocrit is 40, but the white count is 14,400. The urinalysis is normal. You make a tentative diagnosis, put in a central venous catheter, and send him to Radiology for a chest film and supine and upright films of the abdomen (Fig. 34A and B). What is your diagnosis?

ANSWER

The chest film shows an elevated left hemidiaphragm (look at the stomach bubble), left pleural effusion, and left basilar atelectasis. There is no free air under the diaphragm. The abdominal film shows several loops of dilated bowel, probably small bowel, and a possible left epigastric mass indenting the air-filled fundus from below. A single air-fluid level in the right upper quadrant could be in the gallbladder or in the duodenal bulb.

These signs point to an inflammatory mass in the epigastrium and beneath the left diaphragm. A reasonable differential would include acute pancreatitis with an abscess or pseudocyst, a perforated gastric or duodenal ulcer (the free air could be missed if the ulcer perforated into the lesser sac), or possibly a ruptured gallbladder. Here is Mr. Laroche's emergency upper G.I. series (Fig. 34C). Does it help you?

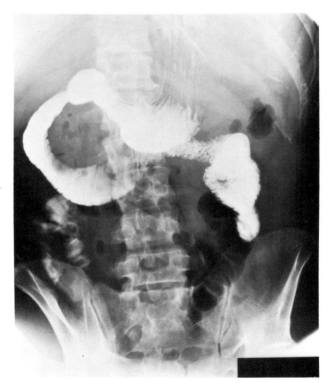

Figure 34 C   A film from the upper G.I. series

ANSWER

It should. The stomach is displaced medially by the mass you have already diagnosed, but in addition, the duodenal sweep is widened and compressed from its medial side by an enlarging mass in or near the head of the pancreas. These are the classic findings in acute pancreatitis, with swelling and edema in the head of the pancreas and a developing abscess or pseudocyst (in the tail of the pancreas). The findings were later confirmed at surgery when the pseudocyst was marsupialized.

CASE 35 AN ELDERLY LADY WITH ABDOMINAL PAIN AND A RIGHT UPPER QUADRANT MASS

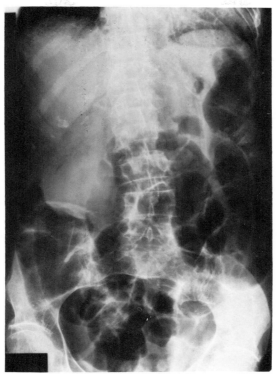

Figure 35   Miss Meddle's abdomen

Miss Mary Meddle, an 84-year-old resident of a nearby nursing home, is sent to you by ambulance because of fever and abdominal distention. No referring diagnosis has been made. Miss Meddle is weak and looks ill, but she is well oriented and is able to tell you that she has had severe midabdominal pain for the past 3 days. The pain has been continuous, but varying in intensity, until today when it became progressively worse, was located more on the right, and was associated with nausea and constipation. She also gives you a history of fatty food intolerance.

Miss Meddle is febrile, with a temperature of 101.4° (po). Her vital signs are otherwise normal, as is the examination of her heart and lungs. Her abdomen is slightly distended and her bowel sounds are diminished. She has definite right upper quadrant tenderness and what you think is a mass beneath the liver. It is difficult to be sure because of guarding. Her white count is 15,000 and her hematocrit 36. The stool guaiac and urinalysis are normal. This is a supine film of her abdomen (Fig. 35). Can you make a diagnosis?

ANSWER

There is a lot of air in her bowel, but it seems to be in both large and small bowel and can be followed around the abdomen and the pelvis.

A more interesting finding is that the air-filled atonic bowel in the right upper quadrant and the fat along the liver edge outline a pear-shaped mass in the right upper quadrant, a distended gallbladder. In this setting it is a reasonable assumption that the gallbladder is distended by bile and an inflammatory exudate. At surgery this proved to be the case. Miss Meddle had acute cholecystitis with hydrops of the gallbladder.

CASE 36 A YOUNG WOMAN WITH ABDOMINAL PAIN AND FEVER

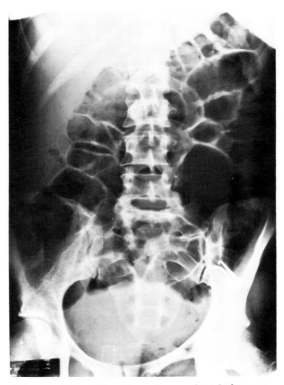

Figure 36   Miss Goodname's abdomen

Miss Adele Goodname is a 20-year-old college student who comes to you with a complaint of abdominal pain and fever of 2 days' duration. She claims to be in good health but in the past 2 days has developed progressive midabdominal pain accompanied by fever as high as 102°. She is constipated. Her symptoms are not worsened by eating, but she has no appetite. She is having a menstrual period.

Miss Goodname looks ill. Her temperature is 101.6° (pr), pulse 80, respiration 22, and blood pressure 112/76. It is difficult to examine her abdomen because of guarding, but there is tenderness over the lower abdomen. Bowel sounds are present but decreased. Her white count is 15,400 with a shift to the left, and her urinalysis shows only a few red cells and epithelial cells. She is very difficult to examine and won't hold still. You send her to Radiology for a plain film of the abdomen (Fig. 36). What is your diagnosis?

ANSWER

There is considerable gas in both large and small bowel yet the pelvis is devoid of gas. Something is keeping the sigmoid colon and the distal small bowel out of the pelvis. In theory this could be a urine-filled bladder, but the patient has already voided for the urinalysis. Uterine or ovarian masses are the next most likely possibilities. Could she be pregnant?

You interview Miss Goodname again. This time she admits that she was pregnant and had gone to an abortionist. Pelvic exam (which really ought to be part of the initial examination of an acute abdomen) confirms the diagnosis of septic abortion with pelvic inflammation. Miss Goodname recovered uneventfully on appropriate therapy.

CASE 37 A GENTLEMAN WITH COLICKY ABDOMINAL PAIN

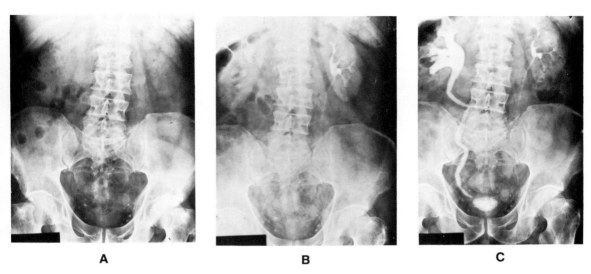

Figure 37 A, B, and C   Mr. Growler's IVP

Mr. Fred Growler, a 65-year-old retired garbage collector, comes to the Emergency Room at three in the morning because of a terrible pain "in the belly." Mr. Growler has had a variety of minor complaints and illnesses, but nothing serious and still drives a cab to supplement his retirement income. However, tonight while watching Betsy Boomer, a lady sportscaster on the eleven o'clock news, he suddenly developed right-sided stomach and back pain, which made him double over in his chair. He got another beer from his refrigerator, but the pain got worse rather than better over the next several hours. The pain is now slightly improved but is felt more in the scrotum than the abdomen, which has Fred even

more worried. He is nauseated, but not vomiting. He has no diarrhea. He urinated at home with no change in the severe pain and no gross blood in the urine. The pain is slightly better now than it was at eleven o'clock.

Mr. Growler's vital signs are normal except for a pulse of 76, and he looks well, if uncomfortable. His abdomen is quiet, but bowel sounds are present. His right flank is tender to soft percussion, but the rest of his abdomen is normal with only voluntary guarding. His CBC is normal. Fred is unable to void. You make a tentative diagnosis and request the appropriate x-rays (Fig. 37A, B, and C). Is your diagnosis correct?

ANSWER

It is correct if you suspected a ureteral calculus with obstruction. The preliminary film shows multiple densities in the pelvis, several of which could be calculi or phleboliths – you can't tell which. The first film from the intravenous pyelogram (Fig. 37B) shows delayed filling of what turns out to be a dilated collecting system on the right. The point of obstruction is shown on the postvoid film (Fig. 37C) to be at the ureterovesical junction, the site at which the calculus has lodged.

Stones usually lodge at one of three areas of narrowing of the ureter: the ureteropelvic junction, the point at which the ureter crosses the iliac vessels, or at the ureterovesical junction.

Mr. Growler's original symptom of flank pain probably began when a calculus from the right renal pelvis lodged at the ureteropelvic junction and obstructed urine flow, causing the right kidney to swell and painfully distend the renal capsule. The 11 P.M. beer may have caused a transient diuresis, helping to force the stone down the ureter to its ultimate lodging place, where the pain was perceived as scrotal.

The absence of *gross* hematuria is not surprising; it is seen in only about one third of cases. Had Fred been able to void, he would certainly have had microscopic hematuria. What else might you have considered in a differential diagnosis of severe acute right flank pain? The following possibilities are reasonable: ureteral calculus, pyelonephritis, renal infarction (especially in a patient with mitral stenosis), appendicitis with a retrocecal appendix, and biliary colic with a stone impacted in the cystic duct.

CASES 38 AND 39 TWO UNUSUAL CAUSES OF ABDOMINAL PAIN

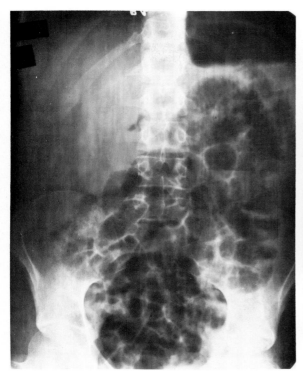

Figure 38 Plummer's abdomen

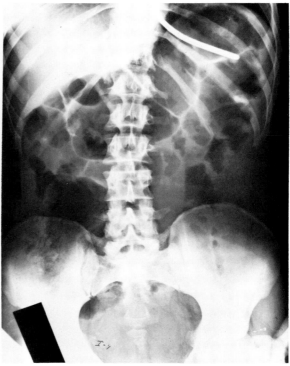

Figure 39 A Darkening's abdomen

Ureteral and biliary colic are two relatively common causes of sudden, sharp, colicky abdominal pain. The next two cases are unusual, though well known, causes of abdominal colic.

Mr. Ronald Plummer (Fig. 38) is a 24-year-old man who has worked in a battery factory for 6 months. He has had intermittent stomachaches and constipation, and for the past 48 hours he has been suffering from colicky pain in his back and abdomen, has been nauseated, and has vomited once. His bowel sounds are decreased, but there is no focal tenderness to palpation of his abdomen. Rectal examination is normal. The white count is 12,000 with a normal differential. His hematocrit is 38 with stippled red cells.

Mr. Donald Darkening (Fig. 39) is a 19-year-old college student with known Addison's disease who has been on steroids for the past 5 years. He has had a "cold" for the past 2 days, first with a sore throat, but now with a nonproductive cough. About 8 hours ago he developed severe abdominal pain, nausea, and vomiting without hematemesis. His vital signs are temperature 98° (po), blood pressure 105/60, pulse 78, and respiration 24. On physical examination, there are normal bowel sounds and there is no focal tenderness and no rebound. His rectal exam is normal and the stool is guaiac-negative. His CBC is normal as is his hematocrit. His serum sodium is 101 mg %. Figure 39B is a chest film to evaluate his cough. What do you make of these two patients?

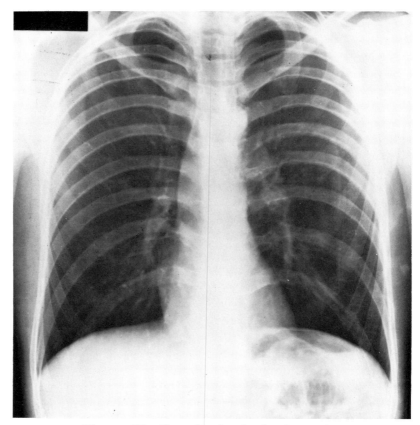

Figure 39   B   Darkening's chest film

ANSWER

Both plain films show a large amount of air in the not overly distended small and large intestine. It would be fair to worry about the pelvic mass in Figure 39A, but that is only the bladder. You've probably made the diagnoses from the histories, which are more useful than the radiographs in these cases. Robert and Donald are suffering from the colicky abdominal pains of lead poisoning and adrenal cortical insufficiency, respectively.

Both conditions are characterized by vague abdominal complaints culminating in episodic abdominal pain (of unknown etiology). Surprisingly, the abdominal examination is relatively normal during an attack and completely normal between bouts of abdominal pain. Donald's chest film shows no pneumonia but the heart is small, possibly owing to the low blood volume.

Incidentally, another possible cause of acute abdominal pain in a patient taking exogenous steroids is a perforated ulcer. That is what Donald's real-life admission diagnosis was. Can you think of any other "medical" causes of acute abdominal pain?

Well, what about sickle crisis or a sickle cell anemia with a splenic infarct, acute porphyria (this may be precipitated by the administration of barbiturates), or Henoch's purpura (in children) with bleeding into the bowel wall? All are well known, if uncommon.

CASE 40   A SCHOOLGIRL WITH LEFT LOWER QUADRANT PAIN AND FEVER

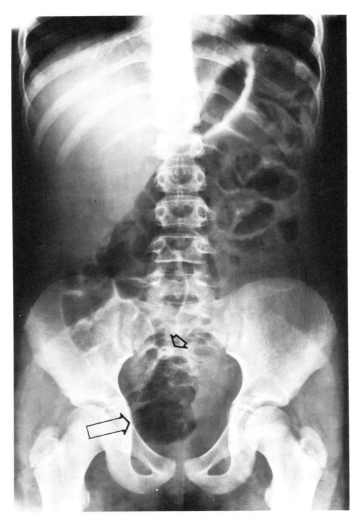

Figure 40   Sissella's abdomen

This intelligent 10-year-old girl, **Sissella Stein,** is brought to the Emergency Room by her parents because of abdominal pain of 24 hours' duration. Her parents are afraid that she has appendicitis. Sissella tells you that the pain was all over her abdomen at first, but is now mainly on the left side. She is nauseated and constipated. Her temperature is 101.6° (po), but her vital signs are otherwise normal. Examination of her abdomen reveals diffuse abdominal tenderness. She has not reached menarche. You do not do a pelvic examination, but on rectal exam there is tenderness and a questionable mass on the left. The white count is 25,800, with 78% polys. She cannot urinate. This is the plain film of her abdomen (Fig. 40); what do you think?

ANSWER

There is a moderate amount of air-filled large and small bowel without any overdistention. The liver looks large but was normal clinically. (Liver size is difficult to evaluate on a plain film; the spleen is easier.)

What about the area of clinical interest, the left lower quadrant? It is devoid of gas as though there were a mass. An appendiceal abscess would be a good statistical probability, but unless the child has situs inversus, the left lower quadrant seems a strange location for an appendiceal abscess. It isn't, though. Look at the short arrow. It points to an appendicolith in the appendix. But what is the appendix doing in the pelvis? Well, that is the ascending colon on the right side of the pelvis with an air-filled cecum sitting just above the bladder (long arrow).

At surgery Sissella had a "mobile" cecum, an inflamed perforated appendix with an appendicolith, and a periappendiceal abscess in the *left* lower quadrant.

CASE 41   A LADY WITH LEFT LOWER QUADRANT PAIN

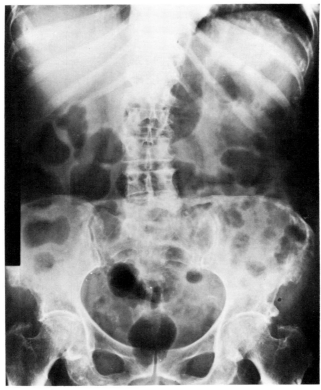

Figure 41 A   Melba Barge's plain film

Melba Barge is a 75-year-old retired opera singer who comes to the Emergency Room with abdominal pain of 2 days' duration. The pain is "all over," she says with great dramatic expression. However, she is able to localize the point of maximum intensity to the left lower quadrant. When you tell her that you have some of her recordings, a bond is established, and Miss Barge confides that she has suffered from intermittent constipation and diarrhea for years, and that she is known to have had diverticulosis. Her constipation has been worse in the past 2 weeks. In the past 3 days it has been accompanied by abdominal pain which was at first midabdominal and steady, but is now located in the left lower quadrant and made worse by attempts at defecation. Miss Barge has not vomited and has not had dark or bloody stools.

Her vital signs are normal except for a temperature of 100° (po). Her white count is 13,400. Urinalysis is normal. Miss Barge is a large, plump lady who seems in good general health. The only positive physical findings are in the abdomen where there is definite left lower quadrant tenderness and rebound, as well as tenderness in the left side of the pelvis on pelvic and rectal examinations. Do the plain films of the abdomen help you (Fig. 41A)?

ANSWER

They help you in that they are essentially normal. There is a mild scoliosis of the spine concave to the left. This could be positional or due to left paraspinal muscle spasm. The abdominal gas is distributed more or less equally throughout the gut from stomach to rectum. There are no masses or calcifications. Do the symptoms suggest a diagnosis or any further avenue of examination?

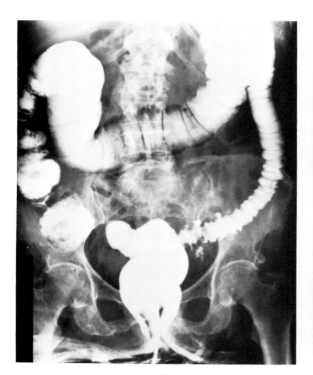

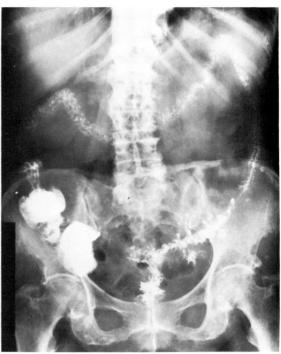

B

C

Figure 41   B and C   Her barium enema

ANSWER

Miss Barge is known to have diverticulosis, not unusual at her age. But diverticulosis alone would not cause her fever and symptoms and signs of inflammation. Diverticulitis would. With a diagnosis in mind, you order a barium enema (Fig. 41B and C). Does it confirm your diagnosis?

Miss Barge has diverticula of the colon, as she has told you. There are at least two dumbbell-shaped diverticula on the superior aspect of the sigmoid. The sigmoid itself appears to have a saw-tooth configuration. This is the result of hypertrophy of the muscularis. These are the findings of diverticulosis.

But there is more, isn't there? There is an irregular collection of barium inferior to the sigmoid, unchanged on both the filled and evacuation films of the colon. This is barium which has extravasated from the colon into a peridiverticular abscess. This is diagnostic of diverticulitis—not surprising, since Miss Barge's symptoms are typical.

Since there was no frank peritonitis, large abscess, or obstruction, Miss Barge was· treated conservatively with antibiotics. She recovered completely.

SECTION VI

Abdominal Pain and Hypotension or Shock

In the presence of hypotension or shock, abdominal pain—even relatively mild pain—takes on greater significance. In the absence of visible blood loss, hypotension is usually due to the loss of fluid into the abdominal cavity: blood from an aneurysm or ectopic pregnancy, or an exudate from peritoneal surfaces inflamed by intestinal juices or by bacterial contamination. Even if there has been loss of blood or fluid from vomiting or diarrhea, there may still be more serious fluid losses elsewhere. Furthermore, in infants and the elderly small losses of fluid volume may prove critical.

Patients who are in shock often need emergency surgery; they usually cannot tolerate repeated radiologic examinations. The plain film becomes exceedingly important. In addition to obvious upper gastrointestinal or lower gastrointestinal hemorrhage, the diagnoses to be considered should include perforation of an ulcer of the stomach or duodenum or of another viscus; cholecystitis; acute pancreatitis; mesenteric infarction; leaking abdominal aortic aneurysm; ectopic pregnancy or septic abortion, or other intra-abdominal abscess.

CASE 42 EPIGASTRIC PAIN AND COLLAPSE

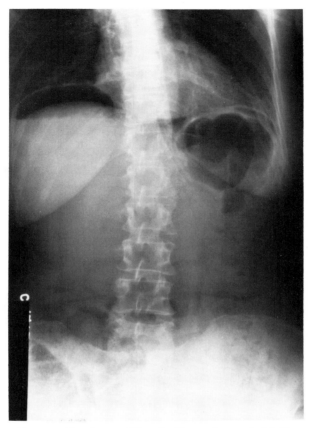

Figure 42 A   Miss LeFevre's upright film

Miss Jacqueline LeFevre (née Elsie McQuade), the 58-year-old owner of an exclusive dress shop, has collapsed in the middle of preparations for her Spring Collection and is brought to your Emergency Room by ambulance.

Miss LeFevre is heavily made-up but clearly in distress, complaining of pain in the stomach. Her blood pressure is 138/70, but her pulse is 90, respiration 24 and shallow, and her temperature 100° (pr). While you examine her, you elicit a history of recurrent indigestion. The indigestion is usually relieved by milk or antacid but recently has been caused by eating.

Today at the dress shop the pain became suddenly worse. At first it was felt in the epigastrium, but now it is felt all over the abdomen. Miss LeFevre has not vomited or had diarrhea, but when asked, she says she has pain at the top of her right shoulder.

The examination of her chest is normal, but the abdomen is not. Bowel sounds are markedly diminished, and the abdomen is firm, almost rigid. There is rebound tenderness all over the right side of the abdomen. Rectal and pelvic examinations are normal with guaiac-negative stools. There is no frank blood in the stomach but the aspirate is guaiac-positive. Do you have a tentative diagnosis? Have a look at the upright film of the abdomen (Fig. 42A).

ANSWER

Obviously there is free air under the diaphragm. There is also some fluid in the peritoneal cavity, since there is an air-fluid level, with the air over the liver. Most of the abdomen is gasless, and there is scoliosis concave to the right, possibly indicating irritation of the right psoas muscle. With this history and physical, and these radiographic signs, you are almost certainly dealing with a perforated duodenal ulcer or, less likely, a perforated gastric ulcer. (The other common source of free air is a perforation of the sigmoid, but we have no signs pointing to that diagnosis.)

Most surgeons would probably take Miss LeFevre straight to the operating room, but in this case the surgeon wanted to localize the perforation. To do this, the radiologist placed Miss LeFevre on her right side and instilled about 40 cc of water-soluble contrast medium by naso-gastric tube (Fig. 42C and D). The contrast fluid has poured out of the duodenal bulb into the right flank, over the liver superiorly and the ascending colon inferiorly.

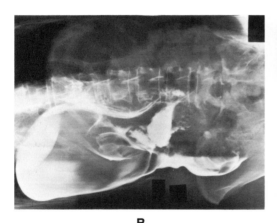

B

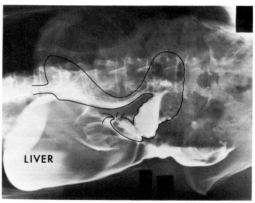

LIVER

C

Figure 42 B and C The decubitus film with Gastrografin

Which decubitus film would you request to show free air? You would put the patient into the *left* decubitus position, since air would then rise into the antrum of the stomach and through the perforated duodenal ulcer to the flank. The left lateral decubitus is the preferred view for any examination for air in the peritoneal cavity for the additional reason that air over the liver is much easier to see than air over the splenic flexure near the stomach bubble.

Miss LeFevre was taken to surgery, and a Billroth II gastrojejunostomy was performed.

CASE 43 PROGRESSIVE ABDOMINAL PAIN
AND HYPOTENSION

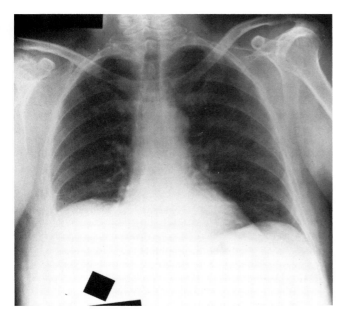

Figure 43 A   Mr. Goodfriend's chest film

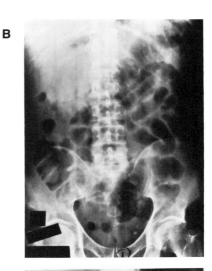

B

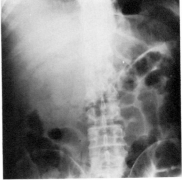

C

Figure 43 B and C   His abdominal films

George Goodfriend, a 67-year-old retired waiter, is brought to the Emergency Room by ambulance with a 4-day history of abdominal pain, nausea, and occasional vomiting. The pain has become worse tonight and is radiating through the back. George is weak and shocky but is able to give a history and says that he has not vomited up any blood or noted any dark stools.

His temperature is 101° (pr), pulse 86, respiration 24 and shallow, and blood pressure 112/74. He has postural tachycardia. The examination of his chest reveals coarse right basilar rales and dullness at the right base. His abdomen is distended without audible bowel sounds. There is exquisite right upper quadrant tenderness and an irregular right upper quadrant mass. The nasogastric aspirate and rectal examination are negative for blood. The white count is 18,000, the hematocrit 48, and the urinalysis normal except for 1+ protein. The serum amylase is considerably elevated at 700 Somögyi units. Here are George's admission chest film and the supine and upright films of his abdomen (Fig. 43A, B, and C).

ANSWER

The chest film is normal except for apparent elevation of the right hemidiaphragm with blunting of the right costophrenic angle. This is due to a combination of diaphragmatic splinting and a subpulmonic effusion. The abdominal films show considerable air in the intestines, but not much fluid. (The only air-fluid level on the upright is in the stomach.) The air-filled bowel outlines the vague right upper quadrant mass you palpated. In addition, the loops of bowel do not sit tightly together, suggesting that there may be fluid free in the abdomen. There is no free air. What is the diagnosis?

The combination of the right upper quadrant mass and a very high amylase and pleural effusion (which also has a high amylase content) along with evidence of hemoconcentration (hypotension and a high hematocrit) should all suggest the possibility of pancreatitis.

Many, if not most, physicians would treat this disease medically with nasogastric suction, anticholinergics, antibiotics, and fluid replacement. This was Goodfriend's initial treatment. However, it was thought possible that the right upper quadrant mass might be an obstructed gallbladder, and an emergency operation was performed in the hope that decompression of the biliary tract would help the pancreatitis. At surgery, there was hemorrhagic pancreatitis with fat necrosis all over the abdomen. The right upper quadrant mass proved to be inflammation around the head of the pancreas.

CASE 44 AN ELDERLY LADY WITH ABDOMINAL PAIN, FEVER, AND HYPOTENSION

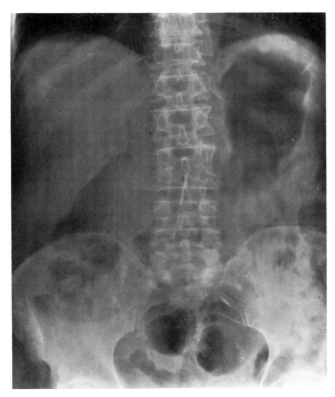

Figure 44 A Mary Duggin's film

Mary Duggin, an 83-year-old ex-chorus girl, now a resident of a nursing home, is brought to you with abdominal pain, fever, and hypotension. She is confused, but between talking to her and to the night nurse at the nursing home (who seems to know nothing of what happened on the day shift) you find out that Mary is diabetic, has not eaten for 3 days, and is nauseated and constipated. She has had intermittent abdominal pain which is localized to the right side. The night nurse gave her some juice this evening, but it was promptly vomited up. Mary's temperature has been slightly elevated and was 102° (po) this evening.

Mary looks seriously ill, with warm dry skin and dry lips. Her temperature now is 101.6° (pr), pulse 80, respiration 20, and blood pressure 132/60. Her cardiorespiratory examination is normal except for a soft systolic ejection murmur. Her abdomen is not distended, but the bowel sounds are diminished and there is marked right upper quadrant guarding and tenderness. Rectal and pelvic examinations are normal. The white count is 15,200 with a shift to the left. The hematocrit is 36. Here is Mary's plain film (Fig. 44A). What is your diagnosis?

ANSWER

It's not a terribly good film, but the abdominal gas pattern is relatively normal, with a gas-filled stomach in the left upper quadrant and gas scattered throughout the rest of the bowel. But wait a minute—what about that pear-shaped collection of gas in the right upper quadrant and what about the faint thin rim of gas around it? These are the findings of emphysematous cholecystitis. Gas-producing bacteria have infiltrated the wall as well as the lumen of the gallbladder. This form of cholecystitis is usually seen in diabetics. Mary was taken to surgery and is now doing well.

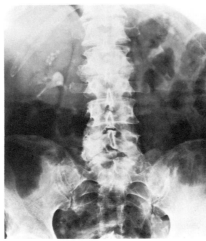

Figure 44 B   The pre-op IVP

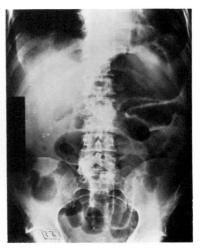

Figure 44 C   The post-op plain film

Now for a fun case. Figures 44B and C are the films of a 73-year-old man who entered the hospital 10 days ago for a prostatectomy. Figure 44B is part of a preoperative IVP which incidentally revealed gallstones projecting over the right kidney. The postop course has been satisfactory, but tonight the patient is complaining of acute midabdominal pain. His abdomen is distended and tympanitic, with no bowel sounds (Fig. 44C). What has happened?

ANSWER

The second film shows ileus, a gasless right upper quadrant, and the gallstones no longer closely bunched together. This could be due to distention of the gallbladder, but in fact it was due to a rupture of the gallbladder. The stones are free in the peritoneal cavity. This radiographic sign is rare, of course. However, postoperative cholecystitis is not rare; it is a well-recognized complication of surgery in the elderly.

CASE 45 AN ELDERLY LADY WITH SUDDEN ABDOMINAL PAIN AND SHOCK

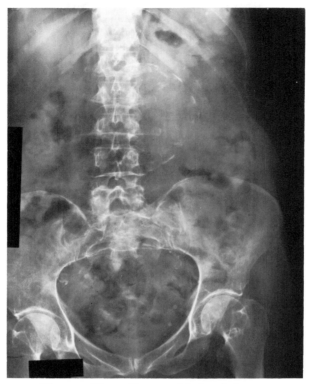

Figure 45   Esmeralda's abdomen

Esmeralda Hyde is an 83-year-old grande dame brought to your hospital complaining of sudden abdominal pain. You know from the newspapers that she has been leading an active life, and she claims not to have been ill a day in her life. Examination of her abdomen reveals diminished bowel sounds. The abdomen is not rigid, and you can feel a large pulsatile mass to the left of the midline. Her hematocrit and white count are normal for her age. Nevertheless, suspecting what this mass might be, you start an IV and personally take her to Radiology for an emergency film of the abdomen (Fig. 45). Are your suspicions correct?

ANSWER

They are. There is a crescent of calcification to the left of the spine. Even though there is a moderate amount of stool in the colon, the upper pole of the right kidney is visible. No renal margins at all can be seen on the left. You slip an intracath into the abdomen and aspirate frank blood which has leaked into the abdominal cavity. Esmeralda goes straight to the operating room for repair of her leaking aortic aneurysm.

CASE 46   ELDERLY LADY WITH ACUTE ABDOMINAL PAIN

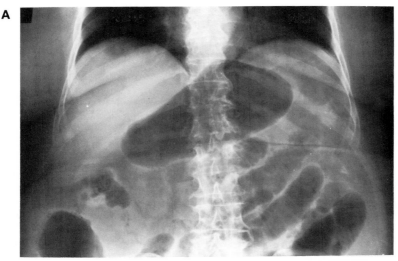

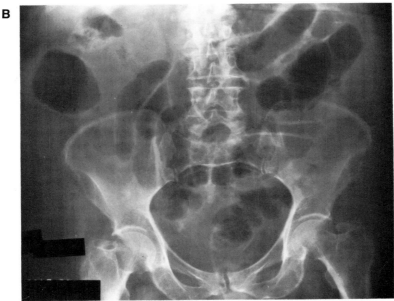

Figure 46   A and B   Annie Bloat's two-part abdominal film

Annie Bloat is another of your nighttime referrals from the local nursing home. Annie is an enormously obese 81-year-old who was admitted to the Medical Service 2 months ago in left ventricular failure. She recovered and was sent back to the nursing home, but she has refused to eat and has become severely dehydrated. She is sent to you obtunded, dehydrated, and complaining of abdominal pain. Her temperature is 100.4° (pr), pulse 78, respiration 16, and blood pressure 130/68.

Examination of Annie's abdomen is difficult because she is so fat and is obtunded. However, the abdomen is tender and there are no bowel sounds. Rectal and pelvic examinations are grossly normal; the hard stool is guaiac-negative. Her hematocrit is 37, the white blood count 14,000, the amylase 100 Somögyi units, and the nasogastric aspirate guaiac-negative. Figure 46A and B is her (2-part) abdominal film. What do you think might be going on?

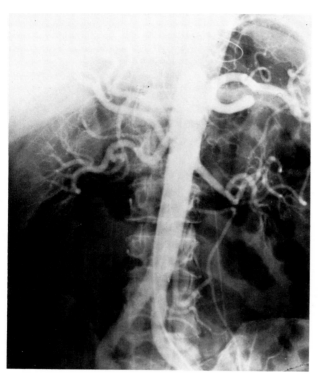

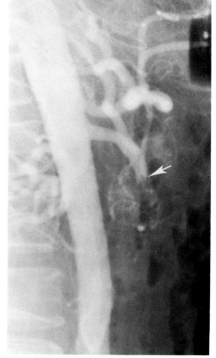

Figure 46 C   AP aortogram   **Figure 46 D   Lateral aortogram**

ANSWER

There is air in the stomach, small bowel, colon, and rectosigmoid, so Annie is probably not obstructed. The small bowel loops in the upper abdomen are dilated out of proportion to the rest of the intestine, though they are not very much distended. Without evidence of obstruction, this implies localized ileus. Could these be sentinel loops with pancreatitis? Possibly, but the amylase isn't really high enough. A septic or ruptured gallbladder, a leaking gastric or duodenal ulcer, or a ureteral stone are all reasonable possibilities. Because of Annie's age, her history of cardiovascular disease, and heart failure you should consider the diagnosis of mesenteric infarction. Figure 46C and D is Annie's angiogram.

The angiogram shows complete occlusion of the superior mesenteric artery about 2 inches from its origin (arrow). At surgery, the bowel was infarcted from the ligament of Treitz to the transverse colon, the distribution of the superior mesenteric artery. Annie died several hours after surgery. Few patients survive extensive mesenteric infarction.

CASE 47   A DIABETIC WITH ABDOMINAL
PAIN AND FEVER

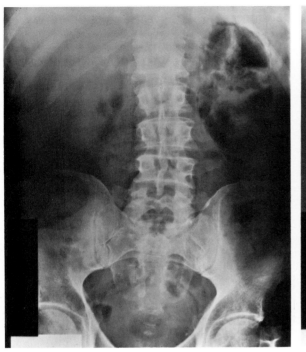

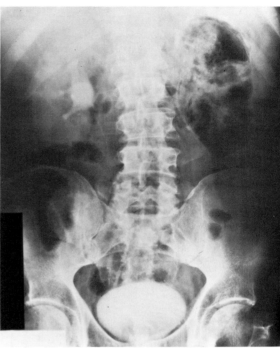

A

B

Figure 47   A and B   McBride's IVP

Joseph McBride is a 62-year-old diabetic brought by his wife to the Emergency Room complaining of abdominal pain. She says that he is becoming rapidly more lethargic and she thinks his diabetes may be out of control.

You find McBride to be somnolent but arousable. He is complaining of pain in the left side of his abdomen and says that it has been worsening for about 2 days. He claims to have taken his insulin and denies any previous gastrointestinal or genitourinary symptoms. His temperature is 101.5° (pr), pulse 78, respiration 22, and blood pressure 126/70.

Although McBride looks ill and has sugar and ketones in his urine, he does not have a ketotic odor to his breath. His blood sugar is 240 mg %, but the serum acetone is negative. The cardiorespiratory examination is normal. His bowel sounds are diminished and there is definite left flank tenderness. Rectal examination is normal. The hematocrit is 39, white blood count 16,000 with a shift to the left, urinalysis 4+ sugar, 1+ ketones, loaded with white blood cells and some red blood cells. What is your diagnosis? Pyelonephritis and diabetic acidosis? That was his real-life diagnosis, at this point. Do the plain films of the abdomen and emergency IVP help you (Fig. 47A and B)?

ANSWER

Well, this is more than simple pyelo-nephritis. The whole left kidney is out-lined and almost replaced by gas. This is renal emphysema due to (Klebsiella) pyelonephritis which has gone out of control and is consuming the kidney. McBride has an uncommon complication of urinary tract infections in the diabetic.

The organism in renal emphysmea is usually Klebsiella or *E. coli*. The im-portant point to note is that the patient's weakness and lethargy is not due to the slightly uncontrolled diabetes but rather to the gram-negative sepsis which must be treated immediately.

McBride was operated on immedi-ately and did well for about a month. Ul-timately, however, he died of Klebsiella pneumonia.

SECTION VII

Abdominal Pain and Distention With and Without Vomiting

In general these symptoms should bring to mind the diagnosis of intestinal obstruction. Vomiting may be seen in almost any abdominal illness, especially in gastritis; however, when distention is also present, the diagnosis of small bowel obstruction must be considered. The point of obstruction may be anywhere from the duodenum to the cecum. Causes of obstruction include postoperative adhesions, gallstones or foreign bodies such as bezoars lodged in the ileum, ileocolic intussusception, and cecal volvulus.

If there is obvious distention or obstruction without any vomiting, especially if there is a history of "constipation," the obstruction may be in the colon, perhaps due to an incarcerated inguinal hernia, a sigmoid volvulus, or an obstructing carcinoma.

The plain film of the abdomen is extremely useful, since in practice the classic high-pitched bowel sounds and rushes may not be heard at first. The radiographic signs to be sought are distended loops of air- and fluid-filled bowel, several or persistent air-fluid levels on the upright or decubitus views, and increasing amounts of air or fluid in one part of the bowel with decreasing amounts of gas in more distal bowel on serial films.

A word of warning: Contrary to popular belief, the normal small bowel contains some swallowed air and occasionally fluid levels. There is more small bowel gas in patients confined to bed and in patients who are in pain.

CASE 48   YOUNG MAN WITH ABDOMINAL PAIN
AND DISTENTION

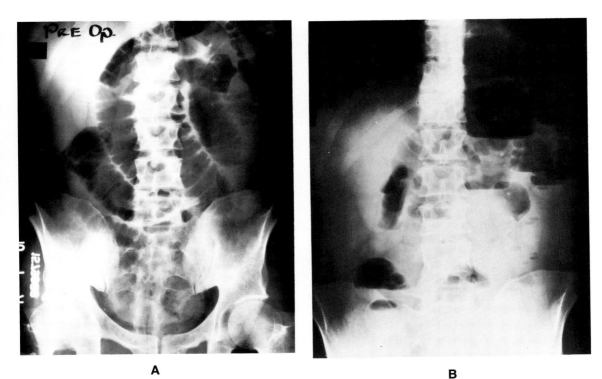

Figure 48   A and B   Peter's supine and upright films

Peter Ping is a 20-year-old Chinese graduate student of philosophy. He comes to the Emergency Room with a 1-day history of vague abdominal pain which has rapidly worsened over the past 12 hours and is now associated with, but not relieved by, vomiting.

Peter is an articulate young man who tells you he is suffering from severe spasms of central abdominal pain. The pain comes in waves but is never completely gone. In the past several hours he has vomited three times. First his vomitus contained his last meal; now he has

dry heaves. His last bowel movement was last night. Peter is in good general health. He had a tonsillectomy 13 years ago and an appendectomy 5 years ago.

Peter's vital signs are normal. He is not febrile and his stool is guaiac-negative, though his rectum is almost empty. His abdomen is slightly distended but soft. The bowel sounds are definitely high-pitched with frequent splashes, gurgles, and pinging sounds. This is Peter's KUB and upright (Fig. 48A and B); his chest film was normal.

ANSWER

Clearly there are multiple loops of dilated bowel shown as parallel air-filled loops on the supine film and as multiple air-fluid levels or pockets of air on the upright. The fluid remains dependent: on the supine film the air rises and lies in the plane of the film outlying the length of the loops; on the upright film the air rises to the apex of the parallel loops while the fluid falls inferiorly. The air-filled apices of the loops are seen very clearly, while the fluid-filled lower portions of the loops become pseudomasses, or pseudo-tumors, in the lower abdomen. The bubbles of air you see are in segments of bowel which are almost completely filled with fluid.

Is this obstruction or ileus? Is it large bowel or small? The history of peri-umbilical pain and vomiting, along with the high-pitched bowel sounds, suggests small bowel obstruction. The radiographs confirm it. These bowel loops are closely packed, coiled together in the mid-abdomen and have frequent transverse plications. This is the appearance of small bowel obstruction.

The ascending and descending colon are fixed and the transverse and sigmoid colon normally have only short mesenteries. Therefore the large bowel does not form these multiple coils. Also, when the colon is distended, it is two to three times the diameter of distended small bowel, and the plications, or haustra, are farther apart. The absence of gas in the colon completes the radiographic appearance of small bowel obstruction.

At surgery Peter was found to have surgical adhesions between the small bowel mesentery and cecum in which the ileum had become trapped. He recovered uneventfully and has decided to become a surgeon instead of a philosopher.

CASE 49   A GRANDMOTHER WITH ABDOMINAL DISTENTION

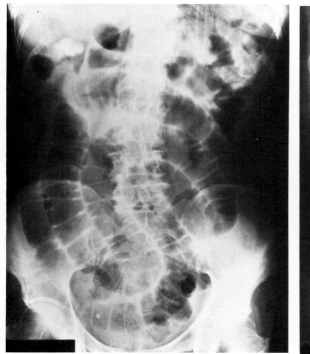

A

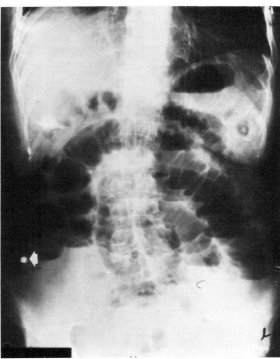

B

Figure 49   A and B   Miss Tinkle's films

Ellen Tinkle is an 80-year-old grandmother who is brought by her family to the Emergency Room because of abdominal pain, distention, and vomiting. Ellen has been in good health, an active member of her household. Her only previous gastrointestinal problem was an episode of pain, vomiting, and light stools 2 years ago which she thought was caused by her daughter-in-law's cooking. Recently her health has been good.

However, during the past week she has been suffering from intermittent abdominal pains which have twice made her vomit. Today she developed persistent pain in the midabdomen and right lower quadrant. She has vomited several times and feels that the vomiting relieves the pain a bit.

Ellen is dehydrated and seems to be in pain. Her temperature is 100.4° (po), pulse 90, respiration 24, and blood pressure 126/90. Her stool is guaiac-negative as is her vomitus. Her hematocrit is 36 and white blood count 13,400 with a shift to the left. Her physical examination is normal for her age except for her abdomen, which is visibly distended and tender throughout. The bowel sounds are definitely increased in amplitude and frequency. Pelvic and rectal examinations are normal. Do the symptoms suggest a diagnosis? Do the signs? What about the supine and upright films of the abdomen (Fig. 49A and B)?

ANSWER

The symptoms, while typical of Ellen's illness, are not very specific. Colicky midabdominal pain, nausea, and vomiting could be due to appendicitis, cholecystitis, biliary colic, ureteral colic, torsion of an ovary, small bowel volvulus, or small bowel obstruction, to pick a few possibilities. The distention, hyperactive bowel sounds, and tenderness are much more useful in narrowing the diagnosis to bowel obstruction. What of Ellen's film?

The small bowel is dilated and coiled in loops in the midabdomen with little or no gas in the colon. There are air-fluid levels on the upright. This confirms your diagnosis of small bowel obstruction, but do you see the reason why the bowel is obstructed? Look in the right upper quadrant. There are several calcified stones in the gallbladder. Now look in the right lower quadrant. There is another stone (arrow) which you might suspect is lodged in the narrow terminal ileum at the ileocecal valve. This is gallstone ileus (obstruction).

Gallstone ileus is a disease of elderly women who often have a history of gallstones or biliary colic, and may have a prodrome of intermittent colic, probably caused by intermittent obstruction as the stone travels to the ileum. The stone usually reaches the small bowel via an inflammatory fistula which has formed between the gallbladder and the duodenum. This duodenobiliary fistula may allow intestinal gas to pass into the biliary radicles in the liver, another sign of gallstone ileus (which is not present in Ellen's case). Incidentally, the calcific density of the stone may be very small on an x-ray. A calcified nidus may be surrounded by a thick uncalcified coating; the stone may be much larger than it looks on an x-ray.

CASE 50   A MIDDLE-AGED LADY WITH ABDOMINAL DISTENTION AND PAIN

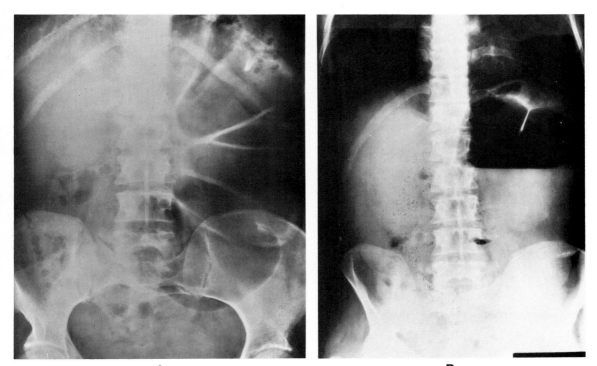

A　　　　　　　　　　　　　　　　　**B**

Figure 50   A and B   Mrs. Groan's supine and upright films

Abdominal pain, vomiting, and distention are **Ethel Groan's** complaints. Mrs. Groan, a 52-year-old housewife, has been in excellent health all her life and felt well until yesterday. During the course of the morning she developed severe abdominal pain and vomited her midmorning snack of chocolate cake and diet soda. She has felt like moving her bowels all day but has been unable to do so. Now she comes to see you in the Emergency Room.

Ethel is clearly in pain and has a slightly distended abdomen. Her pulse is 84, blood pressure 125/85, respiration 18, and temperature 100° (pr). Her bowel sounds are moderately increased and abnormal, with pings, tinkles, groans, and creaking sounds. You can see a poorly defined mass in the epigastrium. Her abdomen is tender but there is no rebound tenderness. Rectal and pelvic examinations are normal. The hematocrit is 42 and the white count 12,000. Urinalysis, stool, and nasogastric aspirate are guaiac-negative. These are the films of Ethel's abdomen (Fig. 50A and B). What is your diagnosis?

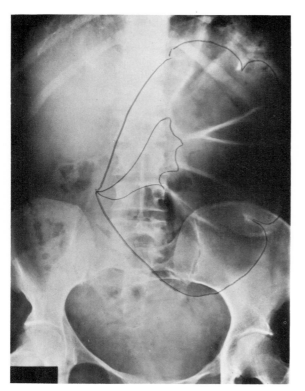

Figure 50 C   The volvulus

ANSWER

There is a large air- and fluid-filled mass filling much of the abdomen. It has what looks like haustral folds and must be dilated gut, probably colon. This is one of those lesions you will recognize much more easily if you have seen one before. Do you get the impression that the bowel is in a loop which is concave toward the right lower quadrant? You could demonstrate that fact by placing Ethel on her left side so that the air would rise to the right. The loop of air-filled bowel would then be defined as it is drawn in Figure 50C. What is the diagnosis? How will you prove it?

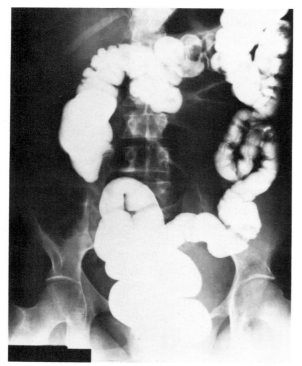

Figure 50   D   The barium enema

ANSWER

Ethel's barium enema (Fig. 50D) confirms the diagnosis. The barium column is blocked at the level of the ascending colon where it terminates in a narrow point, or beak. This is the point of the twist or volvulus of the cecum, Ethel's obstructing lesion. Cecal volvulus is less common than sigmoid volvulus, since the cecum is usually fixed in the right lower quadrant. However, about 15% of patients have a mobile cecum which can flop around and may twist upon itself as it did here.

Ethel's symptoms are not due only to the obstruction of (small) bowel at the level of the cecum. The twist in the cecal mesentery is also certain to have compromised the blood supply to some degree. This and the enormous distention of the cecum are sufficient to account for the symptoms, which are often of sudden onset and rapid progression.

CASE 51 PAIN AND PROGRESSIVE DISTENTION AND VOMITING

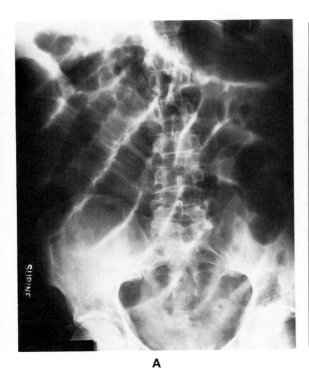

A

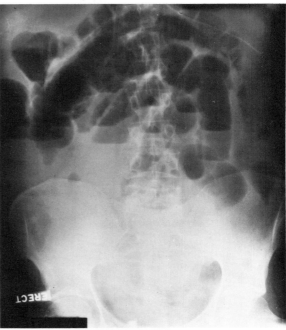

B

Figure 51 A and B   Harold's plain films

Harold Rushes is a 52-year-old magician with a 24-hour history of episodic abdominal pain, distention, and vomiting. He has also had one episode of loose, crampy diarrhea. Harold has been in good health all his life and has had no previous abdominal surgery. Now, however, he is clearly ill and has pain which he says is constant but gets worse from time to time. His vomitus tastes and smells bad, but it is guaiac-negative as is the small amount of stool in his rectum.

Harold's abdomen is clearly distended and, in addition to hyperactive bowel sounds, he has visible peristalsis beneath his abdominal wall. Can you make a diagnosis from his plain films (Fig. 51A and B)?

ANSWER

Clearly the small intestine is dilated; there are multiple loops of air- and fluid-filled bowel. But what is the level of obstruction? There are so many loops that the obstruction must be near the terminal ileum. Would a barium enema help?

A barium enema may make a diagnosis in distal small bowel obstruction either by unmasking what is actually an obstruction of the cecum or proximal colon, or by allowing barium to reflux through the ileocecal valve to outline an ileal lesion. Figures 51C and D are an oblique film from Harold's barium enema and a spot film of the arrested barium column in the right upper quadrant. (Harold could not hold the enema and evacuated before all the films were taken, but use the spot film for diagnosis.)

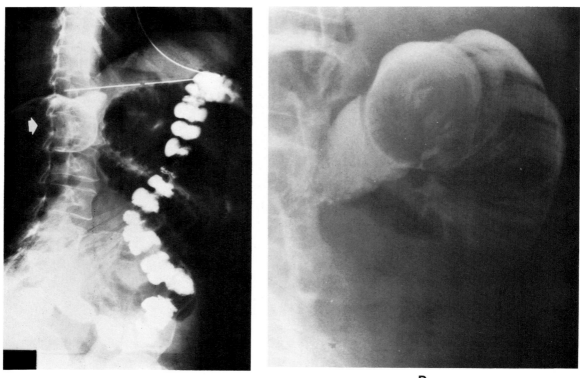

C   D

Figure 51   C and D   Oblique overhead spot film of point of obstruction

ANSWER

Like the twisted C-loop of a volvulus with its beak, this termination of the barium column is unique. It has been described as looking like a "coiled spring" and is so unlike anything else as to be pathognomonic. The spring pattern is caused by barium insinuating itself around a loop of small bowel which has intussuscepted within the colon. This is the typical appearance of an ileocolic intussusception.

In infants this lesion is usually spontaneous, without an underlying pathologic condition. In adults, however, the leading edge of the intussusception is usually formed by a tumor or a Meckel's diverticulum in the ileum. In Harold's case the tumor was a leiomyoma.

Harold was taken to surgery. The intussuscepted small bowel was necrotic and had to be resected, but Harold recovered uneventfully and is now back on the stage, thrilling young and old.

CASE 52 PROGRESSIVE ABDOMINAL DISTENTION WITHOUT MUCH PAIN

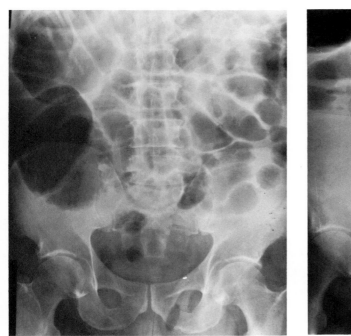 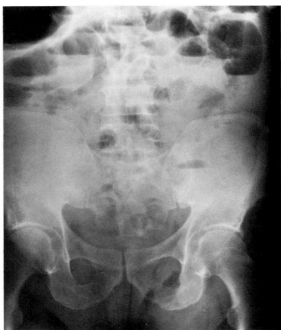

| A | B |

Figure 52   A and B   Maestro Borborygmi's plain films

Alfredo Borborygmi, the 64-year-old conductor of your local symphony orchestra, comes to the Emergency Room on Sunday morning. His complaint is vague abdominal pain, distention, and constipation which has lasted for 2 days and is now making him want to vomit. Alfredo claims to have been in good health all his life and denies any previous gastrointestinal problems. His vital signs are normal, but he is clearly distended and in distress. His abdomen is not tender, but the bowel sounds are increased. Stool guaiac is negative and the CBC is normal. Do Alfredo's plain films help (Fig. 52A and B)?

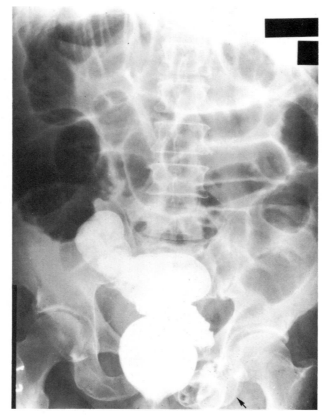

Figure 52   C   His barium enema

ANSWER

There is no question about why his abdomen is distended. There is air-filled, dilated small and large bowel. That large collection on the right is the cecum. But how much of the large bowel is dis-tended? Where is the obstruction? It is hard to say. There is no gas in the rectum or the distal sigmoid, but there are so many loops of bowel that it is difficult to visualize the descending colon which you know should be in the left flank. There is a clue on the film. Do you see it?

ANSWER

There is an inguinal hernia with a loop of sigmoid incarcerated within it.

The gas-filled incarcerated loop is visible on the plain film too.

CASE 53 A LADY WITH "CONSTIPATION" AND DISTENTION

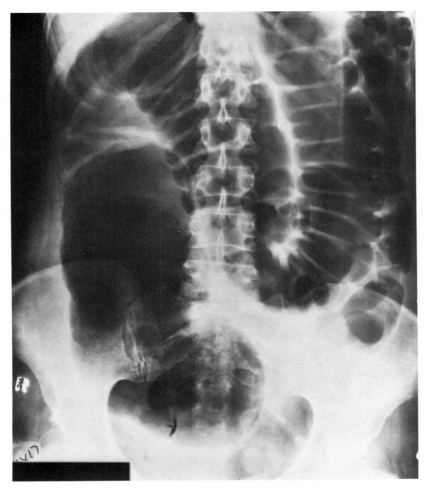

Figure 53 A   Elvira's distended abdomen

Elvira August is a 48-year-old society matron who comes to the Emergency Room with a 3-day history of constipation and a 1-day history of abdominal distention and pain. She has been in good health but recently has suffered from both constipation and diarrhea and has lost about 10 lbs in the past 3 months. When asked, she thinks she tires more easily than in the past but notes no other symptoms.

Mrs. August does not look chronically ill. Her abdomen is visibly distended, so much so that you wonder if she has ascites, but when you examine her you hear hyperactive bowel sounds and note that the abdomen is tympanitic. There are no focal masses. Rectal and pelvic exams are negative, but the stool is guaiac-positive. Mrs. August's hematocrit is 32 and the smear is hypochromic-micro-cytic. Figure 53A is a supine film of Elvira's abdomen. What is your diagnosis?

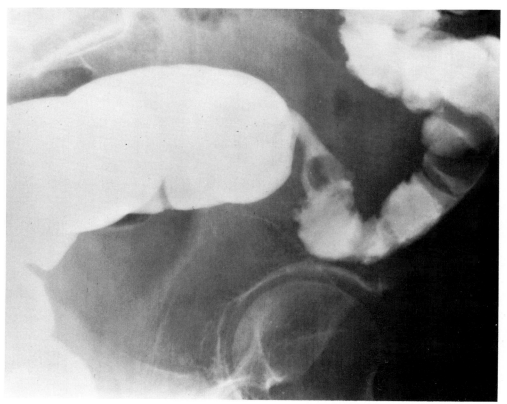

Figure 53   B   Spot film of Elvira's sigmoid

ANSWER

This is large bowel obstruction. The dilated cecum is in the right side of the pelvis. The distended colon can be followed from the cecum up the right flank, down a large "U" of dilated and elongated transverse colon, back to the splenic flexure, and then down the left flank to end near the sigmoid. A spot film from the emergency barium enema (Fig. 53B) shows a narrowed annular, or "napkin ring," carcinoma of the sigmoid almost blocking the flow of barium from the rectosigmoid to the descending colon. The obstruction is antegrade but not retrograde. Probably the acute blockage was due in part to the impaction of firm feces in the narrowed sigmoid. (A lump of feces is visible on the spot film.)

Elvira's presentation is typical. Large bowel obstruction is usually manifest by distention and steady pain. Vomiting is more typical of small bowel obstruction. Blood in the stools, anemia, constipation and/or diarrhea, and local pain and weight loss are the usual symptoms of rectosigmoid carcinoma. Carcinoma of the cecum and right colon rarely obstruct, possibly because the stool remains liquid at that level. Right-sided cancers present as anemia or blood in the stool.

Elvira was taken to the operating room and the carcinoma was resected. If definitive surgery had not been undertaken, the bowel could have been decompressed by an emergency colostomy.

CASE 54 MORE ABDOMINAL DISTENTION

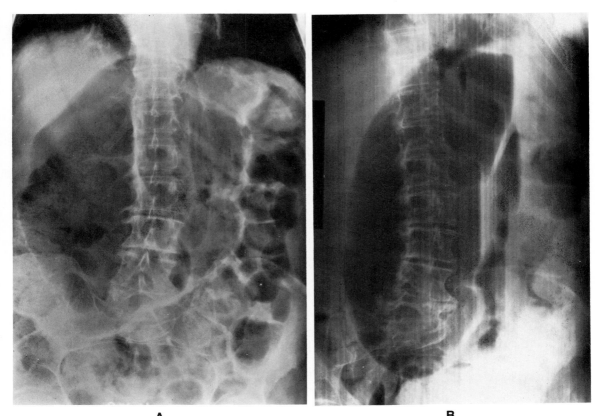

Figure 54 A and B   Mr. Rudenheimer's supine and decubitus films

Rudolph Rudenheimer, a close friend of Annie Bloat, is sent to you by your local nursing home because of abdominal pain and distention. He has been constipated for 4 days and has not had a bowel movement despite having taken several laxatives. Tonight he is complaining of abdominal pain and distention. Rudy is an engaging 71-year-old gentleman who does not look toxic. His vital signs and routine lab work are normal. Stool guaiac is negative. He has no hernias.

Rudy's abdomen is swollen and tympanitic, with hyperactive and high-pitched bowel sounds most noticeable in the left lower quadrant. There are no masses. What do you think of Rudy's supine and decubitus films (Fig. 54A and B)? (The left lateral decubitus is printed upright.)

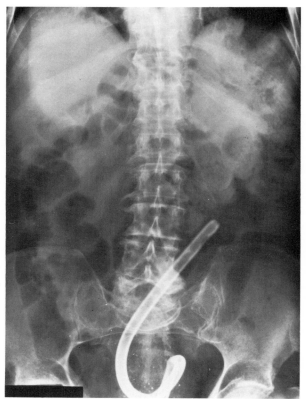

Figure 54 C   Rudy's film after decompression

ANSWER

There is a dilated loop of bowel in the midabdomen, isn't there? Remember that small bowel will not dilate this much. The stomach and colon will. The three most likely possibilities are a dilated stomach, a cecal volvulus, or a sigmoid volvulus. The supine film is not much help except that there seem to be feces and air along the right flank, presumably in the cecum and ascending colon, making a cecal volvulus unlikely. The decubitus film is more useful. The dilated viscus is seen to be in the form of a narrow "C", concave to the left (the opposite of Case 50). The remaining air- and stool-filled bowel is not overdistended. This is volvulus of the sigmoid.

The diagnosis would be definitely proved with a barium enema, but instead it was confirmed another way. The attending house officer performed sigmoidoscopy and, when 25 cm was reached, there was a tremendous gush of wind and liquid feces, which splattered the examiner. The distention decreased visibly and Rudy felt much relieved. A soft rubber catheter was passed into the sigmoid. The followup film (Fig. 54C) now shows Rudy's abdomen in its normal state. (This method of reduction should not be attempted if there are signs of peritonitis.)

CASE 55   A BEDRIDDEN LADY WITH DISTENTION

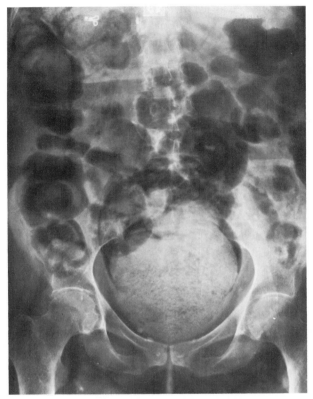

Figure 55   A   Rosalie Sludge's plain film

Rosalie Sludge is another resident of your local nursing home. You have now become well known as a specialist in abdominal distention in the elderly, so when it is noticed that poor Rosalie has not had a bowel movement in 5 days and that her abdomen is swelling, your friends on the night shift at Bedside Manor Nursing Home put Rosalie in an ambulance and send her to see you in the Emergency Room.

Rosalie is a frail, 73-year-old lady who looks a little dehydrated but otherwise well. Her vital signs are normal and lab results are normal for her age. She does have a rather protuberant and tympanitic abdomen. The bowel sounds are slightly increased, but there is no abdominal tenderness. On rectal examination you feel a mass of firm stool which is guaiac-negative. This is Rosalie's KUB (Fig. 55A).

ANSWER

There is gas throughout the bowel but no focal distention. That large mass of granular density in the midpelvis is feces impacted in the rectum and rectosigmoid. It must be removed manually. You send for your medical student.

Feces may become impacted behind an obstructing lesion, but the elderly often get impaction from chronic constipation. Unfortunately, liquid stool may trickle past the impaction, resulting in erroneous treatment for diarrhea.

Impactions are also seen in patients with myxedema or spinal neurologic disorders and in the mentally retarded. Figure 55B is an enormous impaction in a neglected paraplegic from an institution. You can barely make out the spine and pelvis through the feces filling the distended colon. The metallic clips are from previous surgery. An attempt was made to remove the feces surgically, but the patient died.

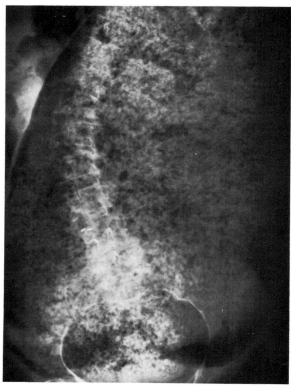

Figure 55   B   A neglected patient

SECTION VIII

Hematemesis

Patients vomiting blood can be a real diagnostic challenge. Take for example the alcoholic who is brought to the Emergency Room vomiting up large amounts of bright red blood. He could be bleeding from varices, gastritis, a duodenal ulcer, or an esophageal tear. Any of these would be a likely diagnosis in such a patient. The history may be nonspecific. A common presentation of upper G.I. bleeding is the patient with vague, indigestion-like pains who suddenly has a large black bowel movement, feels weak and faint, and vomits blood. Presumably the blood in the G.I. tract acts as a cathartic, and the passing of a stool, followed by standing up, makes the patient weak and nauseated. Of course, the history may be much more specific. Vomiting may precede hematemesis for some time, suggesting a Mallory-Weiss tear of the esophagus, for example. The patient may have the stigmata of portal hypertension, increasing the likelihood of variceal bleeding.

The first thing to do is stabilize the patient and quantitate the bleeding. Next, consider which method to use to make the diagnosis. If the hemorrhage is massive and cannot be stopped, the patient must go straight to surgery or, in some centers, to Angiography for selective infusion of Pitressin. If the bleeding is brisk, but the patient is stable, you may want to consider emergency gastroscopy. On the other hand, if the bleeding is slight, an emergency upper G.I. series may be the quickest and easiest way to make a diagnosis. In patients who have only a *history* of hematemesis, you may wish to empty the stomach by suction, or by placing the patient NPO, before obtaining an upper G.I. series the next day, when the stomach is completely empty. The mucosal detail obtained in the examination of an empty, "dry" stomach is considerably better than that obtained of a stomach which still has residual blood and secretions within it.

CASE 56   AN ALCOHOLIC VOMITING BLOOD

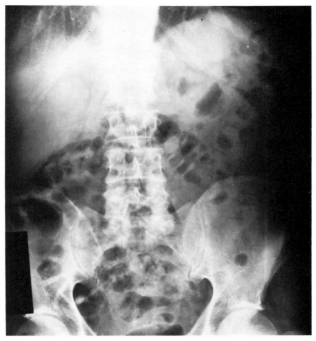

Figure 56   A   Roscoe's plain film

Roscoe Reddy is a 56-year-old alcoholic known to you in the past. He is usually brought in by the police to be examined before being sent to the state hospital for alcoholism to "dry out." This time, however, Roscoe is in bad shape. He is vomiting large amounts of bright red blood and is shocky, with cool, moist skin, a blood pressure of 110/62, and a pulse of 84. His hematocrit is 31.

As you're putting in an IV, you examine Roscoe and take a history. He says he has been having stomach pains for several months, usually made worse by drinking and better by eating. His bowel movements have been tarry for the past 2 days. Today, while on the street, he suddenly felt weak and vomited up a mouthful of blood. A companion called the police. Roscoe has been drinking up until today. He has not had the DT's for several months. This is Roscoe's plain film of the abdomen (Fig. 56A).

ANSWER

The plain film is not very helpful. It is normal. The nasogastric tube is not in the stomach and was, in fact, coiled in the esophagus. There is no evidence of ascites and no gross splenomegaly, but much of the spleen is obscured by air in the small bowel. There was no free air on the decubitus film.

In spite of 4 units of whole blood, Roscoe is still not stable. His pulse is elevated and he still looks pale and sweaty. Bright red blood is coming from the nasogastric tube and he has passed a maroon stool. What will you do next?

ANSWER

If you are in a large hospital, you have several options. An emergency upper G.I. series may tell you that Roscoe has varices, but with a large amount of blood in the stomach, examination of the stomach and duodenum is likely to be limited. Esophagogastroscopy will also allow visualization of varices, but if there is a large amount of blood, you may see little in the stomach unless there is a large ulcer. On the other hand, esophagoscopy is the only good method of visualizing a Mallory-Weiss tear of the distal esophagus. You could also put down a Blakemore tube and attempt to tamponade bleeding varices as a diagnostic trial.

You decide to send Roscoe to Angiography, since he is still bleeding briskly and is likely to need emergency surgery. Since Roscoe's symptoms suggest a duodenal ulcer, the angiographer first catheterizes the hepatic branch of the celiac axis. Injecting this, he visualizes the liver, the gastroduodenal artery to the duodenum, and the gastroepiploic artery running along the greater curvature of the stomach. Figures 56B and C are frames from the angiogram during the arterial phase and after the contrast has left the veins and dissipated into the blood pool. Can you make a diagnosis?

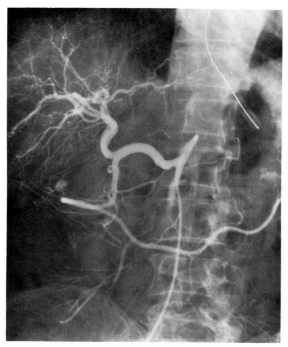

Figure 56   B   Arterial phase

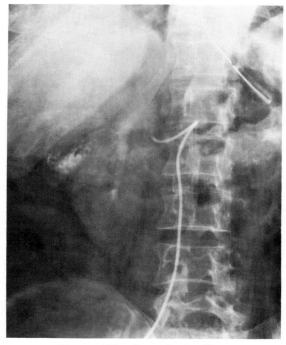

Figure 56   C   Late film

ANSWER

Yes, you can. Contrast is leaking from some of the smaller branches of the gastroduodenal artery. The contrast remains in the duodenal bulb on the late film. Since Roscoe is a reasonably good surgical candidate, has had a major bleed, and is unlikely to stick to medical treatment, he is taken to the operating room where a gastrojejunostomy is performed.

CASE 57   ANOTHER ALCOHOLIC WITH HEMATEMESIS

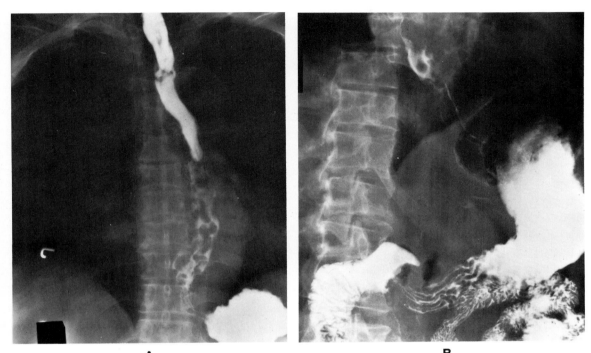

A　　　　　　　　　　　　　　　　**B**

Figure 57   A and B   Freddy's previous upper G.I. series

Freddy Reddy is Roscoe's brother. He too suffers from alcoholism and has known varices. Figures 57A and B are two films from Freddy's last upper G.I. series showing multiple large serpentine filling defects in the distal esophagus and a grossly normal stomach and duodenal bulb.

Freddy is brought to your emergency room in a state of collapse vomiting large amounts of blood. Two hours after admission you have used up 6 units of blood and Freddy is still bleeding. You call the angiography team in the hope that they can localize or control the bleeding. Here is what they do.

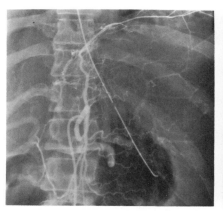

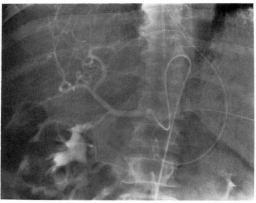

Figure 57 C   Left gastric artery injection

Figure 57 D   Hepatic artery and gastroduodenal artery

A catheter with a curved tip is slipped through a large-bore needle into the femoral artery and advanced up the aorta to the celiac axis, from which the vessels to the stomach, duodenum, spleen, and liver arise. First the left gastric artery is selected and contrast injected (Fig. 57C). No extravasation is seen. Next the hepatic artery, with its major branch the gastroduodenal artery, is injected (Fig. 57D). Again, there is no extravasation. (Notice that the contrast in the renal pelvis could obscure a small bleed unless the patient is rotated.) So, there is no evidence of bleeding gastritis or gastric or duodenal ulcer. What about bleeding varices?

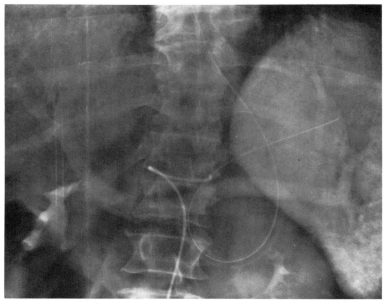

Figure 57   E   Venous phase of splenic injection

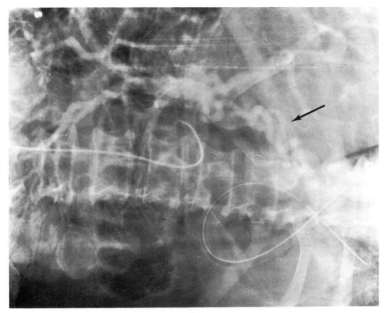

Figure 57 F Venous phase of superior mesenteric injection showing varices (arrow)

Gastroesophageal varices are dilated veins which decompress the portal system by connecting the splenic or portal veins with the systemic veins of the stomach and esophagus. They ultimately empty into the hemiazygous system and the superior vena cava. The point to remember is that they are *veins* and that the angiographer is in the *arterial* side of the vascular tree. It will be impossible to get enough contrast into the veins to see extravasation; it may be difficult even to demonstrate varices. So, the angiographer tries to demonstrate evidence of portal hypertension. He injects a large amount of contrast into the splenic artery and the superior mesenteric artery. The contrast will traverse the capillary bed and return in the splenic and superior mesenteric veins. The angiographer looks for abnormal channels (varices) or ab-

normal patterns of blood flow (away from the liver) indicating portal hypertension.

The venous phases of Freddy's angiograms (Fig. 57E and F) actually show the tangle of varices extending from the coronary vein, near the origin of the portal vein, toward the esophagus.

Next, the angiographer attempts to stop the variceal bleeding by infusing a vasoconstrictor, Pituitrin, through the catheter into the superior mesenteric artery. By reducing blood flow into the artery, he reduces venous flow back through the superior mesenteric vein and thereby decreases the amount of blood flowing into the varices, decompressing them.

This Pituitrin infusion was successful. Freddy was stabilized and underwent an elective portocaval shunt 3 days later.

CASE 58 A "SOCIAL" DRINKER WITH HEMATEMESIS

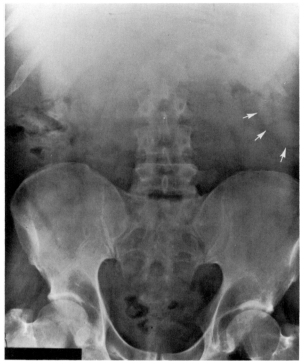

Figure 58 A   Captain Yorking's abdomen

Edward Yorking comes to you because he has vomited blood. Mr. Yorking is a 52-year-old retired Merchant Seaman who lives with his sister. For about a month he has had stomach pains which are relieved by food or milk and made worse by alcohol. His sister says he drinks, but he claims he drinks no more now than he used to, about two highballs a day with his friends. This afternoon he felt nauseated and vomited up his lunch along with coffee-ground material.

Edward looks well. He has a ruddy complexion but no palmar erythema and no spider angiomas on his trunk. There is no evidence of ascites or hepatomegaly, but the tip of his spleen is palpable. His vital signs are normal. However, his stools and nasogastric aspirate are both guaiac-positive, though there is no red blood in his stomach. His hematocrit is 38. How will you handle him?

There is no doubt that Mr. Yorking has been bleeding from his upper gastrointestinal tract. However, he is not hemorrhaging and seems to be a healthy man who will not get into trouble very fast if he starts bleeding again. On the other hand, his KUB (Fig. 58A) confirms that his spleen is enlarged (arrow) so he may have portal hypertension and varices.

You decide to empty his stomach by suction and obtain an emergency upper G.I. series. Figures 58B, C, and D are views of Edward's esophagus, stomach, and duodenal bulb. Why is he bleeding?

B

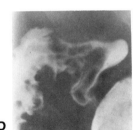

D

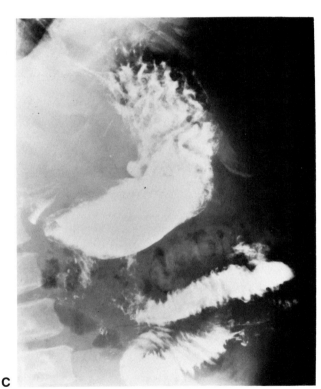

C

Figure 58 B and C   Yorking's upper gastrointestinal tract

ANSWER

He does have varices, but he has a second lesion—a smooth, round ulcer projecting beyond the lesser curvature of his stomach (Fig. 58C). The ulcer has a smooth collar of edematous mucosa around it and the mucosal folds run up to the ulcer on the overhead view. This proved to be a benign gastric ulcer as you would expect from its appearance. The duodenum is normal.

Only about 50% of patients with varices and hematemesis are actually bleeding from the varices. The majority of the rest are bleeding from ulcers, gastritis, or esophageal tears.

CASE 59 HEMATEMESIS AT THE END OF A BINGE

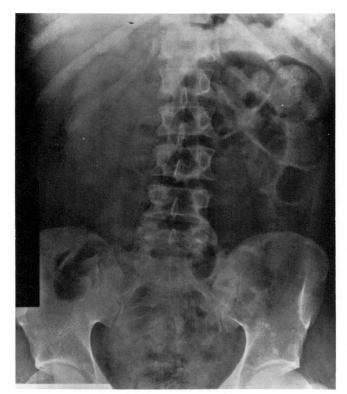

Figure 59   A   Armitage Presser's abdomen

Armitage Presser is a 42-year-old foreign correspondent who is in town for his college reunion. Armitage claims to be in excellent health, but it sounds as though he has drunk his way through every Press Club in Asia. Reunion Week has been one long binge. He comes to the Emergency Room this evening with persistent epigastric pain, vomiting everything he tries to get down. The last episode of vomiting and heaving brought up about a cupful of bright red blood.

Armitage is dressed for the part, complete with college blazer and his name on a lapel tag, but he is a little gray under his suntan and is clearly in pain. His blood pressure is 128/82, pulse 74, respiration 16, and temperature 98.4° (po). He does not have postural hypotension and his hematocrit is 40. The aspirate is coffee-ground and guaiac-positive. Except for epigastric tenderness without rebound, his physical examination is normal. His chest film is normal. Figure 59A is his KUB. How will you handle him?

ANSWER

The abdominal film is normal. There is no evidence of hepatomegaly or splenomegaly, and the abdominal gas pattern is normal. Clinically, Armitage has a good story for alcohol-induced gastritis, but he is not hemorrhaging at the moment. Unless he bleeds uncontrollably, his treatment will be rest, nasogastric suction, and antacids. You could simply watch him and do nothing, which is probably what he would have done if he were on an assignment, or if he hadn't vomited blood. You could also perform gastroscopy or obtain an upper G.I. series to confirm the diagnosis of gastritis. Both gastroscopy and barium studies were performed. Have a look at the G.I. series (Fig. 59B and C) and try to predict what the gastroscopy showed.

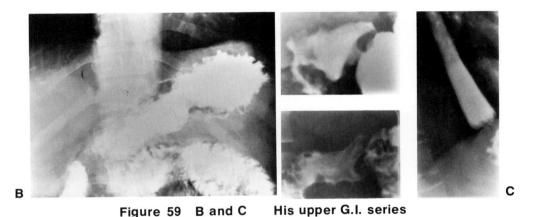

Figure 59 B and C   His upper G.I. series

ANSWER

The esophagus and duodenal bulb are normal. The stomach is not. The barium coats the mucosa poorly because of excess mucus and blood. The gastric folds are heaped up or thickened. Thickened folds and excess mucus with blood are precisely what was found at gastroscopy, along with diffuse hyperemia and superficial erosions which were oozing a small amount of blood. In reality, of course, the emergency gastroscopy was done before the upper G.I. series, since barium would spoil the gastroscopy.

Armitage was put to bed and at first did well, but on the second hospital day his symptoms recurred and he began to vomit up large amounts of blood. After requiring 8 units of blood he was taken to the Angiography suite and his left gastric artery was catheterized (Fig. 59D and E, page 130). Residual barium from the upper G.I. series is in the colon. What do you make of the angiogram?

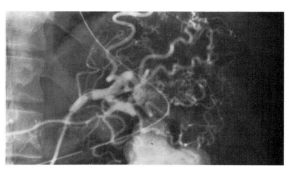

D

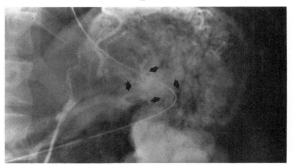

E

Figure 59   D and E   The left gastric arteriogram

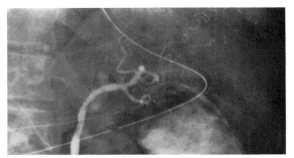

Figure 59   F   After Pituitrin was infused

ANSWER

The angiogram shows the large and small gastric vessels to be dilated. Moreover, there is extravasation of contrast (arrows) which appears on the early film and persists on the late film (arrows). Next, the left gastric artery was infused with surgical Pituitrin. Figure 59F shows the marked constriction of the gastric vessels. The bleeding stopped. After 24 hours the infusion was stopped and the catheter was removed. Armitage made a complete and uneventful recovery. Before this method of treatment was available, he would probably have had a subtotal gastrectomy.

SECTION IX

Bloody Diarrhea and Rectal Bleeding

Red blood in the stool is almost always due to a lesion in the large bowel. Rapid bleeding from the terminal ileum, as from a Meckel's diverticulum, may result in bloody stool, but colonic lesions are the usual cause of frank blood in the stool. The bloody diarrhea of upper gastrointestinal hemorrhage is mixed with digested (black) blood and is rarely confused with lower gastrointestinal hemorrhage.

Bloody diarrhea and rectal bleeding almost always indicate serious disease. Diagnoses to be kept in mind are bleeding diverticulosis, carcinoma, ulcerative colitis, mesenteric infarction, intussusception, and bleeding Meckel's diverticulum. Anorectal hemorrhoids may occasionally hemorrhage, and the blood loss may be life-threatening, as for example when the internal hemorrhoids of a cirrhotic patient burst.

Sigmoidoscopy or proctoscopy are the first logical steps after the history and physical have been completed. The radiologic approach will depend on the severity of the bleeding, as in the case of upper gastrointestinal hemorrhage. Plain films should always be obtained. A barium enema is often diagnostic, but if it is not, residual barium in the colon may make the angiographic identification of extravasated contrast impossible. For this reason, some centers refer the patient with rectal *hemorrhage* to Angiography immediately following the plain film.

CASE 60   A LADY LAWYER WITH BLOODY DIARRHEA

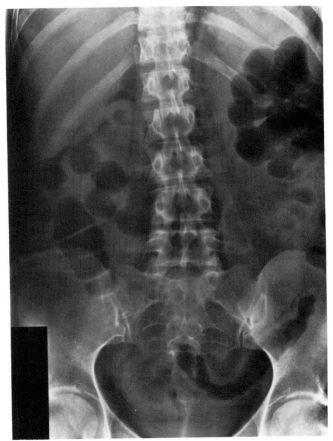

Figure 60   A   Atty. Dorothy Rumble

Dorothy Rumble, a 34-year-old lady trial lawyer, comes to the Emergency Room one afternoon because she is having bloody diarrhea. Atty. Rumble was in good health until about a month ago when she began to have irregular bowel movements with both constipation and diarrhea. The diarrhea has become more frequent, and in the past two days has increased to 4 to 5 bowel movements a day and 2 to 3 bowel movements a night. In addition, she is now having severe lower abdominal and rectal pain with each movement. There may have been some blood on her stool previously, but today she has reddish stool and there is frank blood in the toilet.

Ms. Rumble has a temperature of 99.2° (po), but her vital signs, CBC, and urinalysis are normal. Physical examination is normal except for tenderness on palpation of the left lower quadrant. You attempt sigmoidoscopy but are unable to complete the examination because of pain. What rectal mucosa you see is inflamed. Figure 60A is Ms. Rumble's abdominal film.

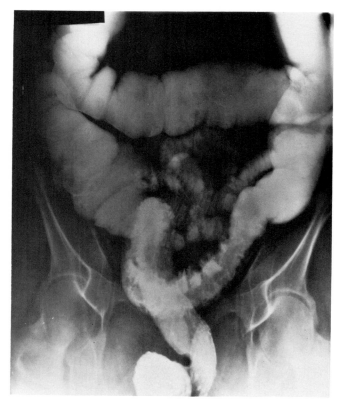

Figure 60   B   Ms. Rumble's enema

ANSWER

The KUB is almost normal. However, that length of air-filled bowel in the left lower quadrant should bother you. The sigmoid usually collapses if it is not filled with feces or ballooned up with air. Moreover, this long segment of bowel has an irregular margin. It may be thickened and stiffened by edema or blood in the bowel wall.

Ultimately, both sigmoidoscopy and barium enema were successfully completed (Fig. 60B). What do you think was seen?

At sigmoidoscopy the mucosa was bloody, edematous, swollen, and covered with mucus. There were mutliple ulcers, some of which were confluent, leaving islands of mucosa which looked like cobblestones. These findings are reflected in the barium enema (look at the sigmoid). The poor coating of the mucosa by the barium is due to the excessive mucus and blood, the nodularity is caused by edema and cobblestoning, while the pointed spicules represent barium in the ulcer crypts. This is ulcerative colitis.

Sometimes the sigmoidoscopic findings are difficult to interpret, while the radiographic findings are more typical or more representative of the disease. Even if sigmoidoscopy is diagnostic, a barium enema is needed to show the extent of the disease in colon beyond the range of the sigmoidoscope.

CASE 61 YOUNG GIRL SERIOUSLY ILL WITH SEROSANGUINEOUS DIARRHEA

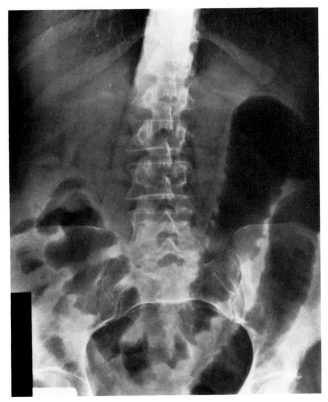

Figure 61 Penelope Pristine

Penelope Pristine is a 25-year-old graduate student working for her Ph.D. in philosophy. She has had diarrhea off and on for about 2 months and was told by her family doctor that she has "colitis." She comes to the Emergency Room now with a 10-day history of severe diarrhea which has been serosanguineous for 24 hours. She is now having little diarrhea, but feels very ill and has a temperature of 102° (po).

Penelope looks sick. She is thin, pale, and dehydrated. In addition to the fever, she has tachycardia, but her blood pressure is normal. Her abdomen is slightly distended and diffusely tender with a sensation of a mass across the mid-abdomen. There is no rebound. Bowel sounds are diminished. Her hematocrit is 30 and white count 13,000 with a shift to the left. The stool is watery and bloody. You make a clinical diagnosis of acute ulcerative colitis and send her for films of the abdomen. Is your diagnosis correct?

ANSWER

Figure 61 is the supine plain film of the abdomen showing the transverse and sigmoid colon to be air-filled and dilated. The air outlines an irregular mucosal border (in the distal transverse colon) into which what seem to be flat-headed polyps protrude. These are not true polyps, though; the intestinal gas is actually outlining "collar-button" ulcers which are undermining the mucosa, forming pseudopolyps.

The dilatation of the colon, along with Penny's toxic appearance, are the ominous findings of toxic megacolon. This complication of ulcerative colitis may occur at any time, though usually is seen in acute fulminating ulcerative colitis. The acutely inflamed colon is thin, dilated, and friable. It has been described as being like wet blotting paper. A barium enema (which you hadn't requested) is clearly contraindicated, since it might perforate the colon.

The amount of blood loss is likely to be far less than the fluid and electrolyte loss. Though the diarrhea is copious, it is watery and exsanguinating bleeding is unlikely.

Patients with toxic megacolon may perforate the colon and may die if not treated immediately. Penny is much more seriously ill than was Dorothy Rumble.

CASE 62 SUDDEN ABDOMINAL PAIN AND BLOODY DIARRHEA

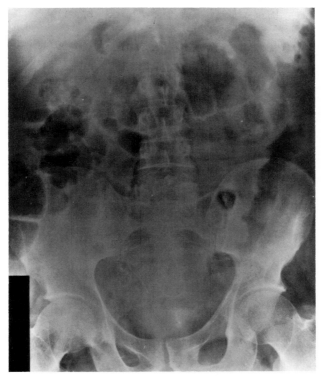

Figure 62 A   Dunstan's plain film

Dunstan Wood is a 65-year-old retired Shakespearean actor who comes to the Emergency Room following the sudden onset of bloody diarrhea and abdominal pain. Mr. Wood is a diabetic with severe peripheral vascular disease and coronary artery disease. This evening, he was awakened from his sleep by severe lower abdominal pain which was accompanied by the urge to defecate. His stool is grossly bloody.

He is weak and in pain, but not in shock. Cardiorespiratory examination is normal except for cardiac enlargement and atrial fibrillation. His abdomen is quiet with few bowel sounds. The left lower quadrant is tender. Proctoscopic examination shows thick, purplish mucosa with multiple small bleeding points. His hematocrit is 40 and white count 12,500 with a normal differential. Figure 62A is his KUB. What do you think of it?

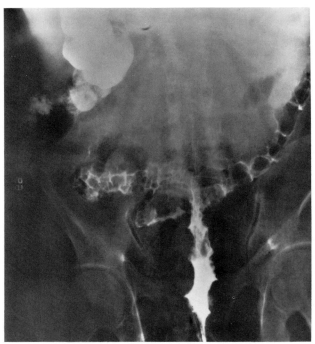

Figure 62   B   A view from the enema

ANSWER

There is gas throughout the abdomen without any focal dilatation. Parts, at least, of the psoas margins are visible. Without decubitus and flank films it is impossible to be sure about free fluid or free air. His symptoms and signs point to the left lower quadrant: what about that long segment of descending colon and sigmoid? It is partially filled with air which outlines a scalloped bowel wall. It looks very like the thickened edematous sigmoid in Case 60, doesn't it? The subsequent barium enema (Fig. 62B) shows this "thumbprinting" of the colon even better. It is due to edema and hemorrhage in the bowel wall and it is typical of colonic infarction, in this case due to sudden occlusion of the inferior mesenteric artery by an embolus.

Collateral blood vessels from the superior mesenteric artery via the marginal artery usually allow the distal large bowel to recover without need for surgical intervention.

CASE 63 PAINLESS RECTAL HEMORRHAGE

Eva Mudge is a 69-year-old grandmother. She has a long history of intermittent constipation relieved by laxatives. However, in the past several weeks her constipation has been worse than usual. This evening, after moving her bowels, she felt the need for another movement. It was grossly bloody and was followed by two more movements which were liquid and bloody. She feels faint, but has no abdominal pain. Her children bring her to the Emergency Room.

Mrs. Mudge's vital signs confirm the blood loss. Her blood pressure is 115/75 and her pulse 84. Temperature and respiration are normal. She is a plump, well-hydrated lady, but her skin is pale and sweaty and she looks anxious. Her chest and cardiac examinations are normal. Her abdomen is obese and soft, with slight right lower quadrant tenderness. The bowel sounds are hyperactive but normal in quality. She's still bleeding profusely per rectum. Her hematocrit is 29. The nasogastric aspirate is guaiac-negative. After 5 units of blood in a 3-hour period, her hematocrit is only up to 36 and she still has tachycardia. Her KUB and upright, and chest film (not shown), are normal. What will you do next?

ANSWER

You haven't really stabilized Mrs. Mudge, and with this much blood replacement you must consider taking her to the Operating Room for an exploratory laparotomy and colotomy. Another alternative is to try to localize the bleeding angiographically. She is bleeding briskly, and the site of extravasation should be visible, since focal bleeding at a rate of about 2 cc per minute is usually detectable.

The most common cause of massive acute lower gastrointestinal hemorrhage in this age group is a bleeding diverticulum of the colon. With any luck, the angiographers should be able to localize the bleeding point and may be able to stop the bleeding by infusing a vasoconstrictor into the bleeding vessel. Surgery will then be either simplified or obviated. Figure 63 is a frame from the superior mesenteric angiogram. Where is the bleeding coming from?

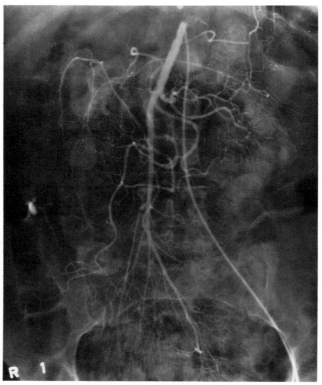

Figure 63   **Mrs. Mudge's superior mesenteric angiogram**

ANSWER

It is coming from the right colon (probably from a branch of the ileocolic artery), isn't it? Although diverticula are more common in the sigmoid and the left colon, they often seem to bleed from the right colon. We don't know why.

SECTION X

Vomiting

The stimuli which result in vomiting may originate in the cerebral cortex, the brainstem, the inner ear, any hollow viscus, the diaphragm, or the peritoneum. Radiology is most useful in cases of gastrointestinal disease. In general, vomiting which is related to the ingestion of food or liquid is likely to be due to an organic gastrointestinal lesion. Vomiting unaccompanied by nausea is more likely due to a CNS lesion. Psychogenic vomiting may be difficult to diagnose.

Adults, unless they have become unconscious or are severely debilitated, can usually give a history of localized pain or associated symptoms which suggest the diagnosis. In the absence of a good history, the most useful information is the time between eating (or feeding) and vomiting. Immediate vomiting suggests an esophageal lesion. Vomiting shortly after meals suggests a duodenal or pyloric lesion. Vomiting between meals may be due to small bowel obstruction.

In young children one must always consider the possibility that the child has a CNS lesion, such as meningitis, or that he has ingested a poison.

CASE 64   PERSISTENT VOMITING

Mary Sunshine is a 16-year-old student at a local boarding school. She is sent to your Emergency Room by her school nurse who has discovered that she has been vomiting off and on for the past several weeks. Mary insists that there is nothing wrong with her. The Emergency Room nurse suggests that you obtain Mary's lab results and x-rays before you see her, since you are busy. You agree. Here is the plain film of her abdomen.

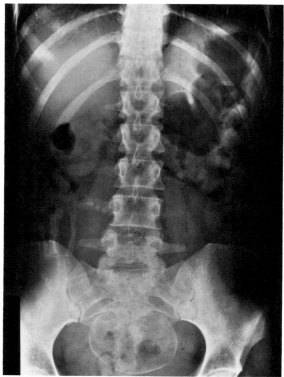

Figure 64   Mary Sunshine's KUB

ANSWER

Yes, that is a fetus. The head is in the pelvis. Most of its spine overlies vertebrae, but you can see the bones of the legs to the right of the spine. Ordinarily the fetal skeleton is calcified sufficiently to be seen on x-rays by about 17 weeks.

The particulars of this case are fictional, but this film actually was obtained without knowing that the patient was pregnant. This fetus is about twenty-six weeks of age and has passed the stage of maximum sensitivity to radiation, which is approximately 2 weeks to 2 months of fetal age. We think that the radiation dose to the fetus, even in these early stages, is small; nevertheless, it is safer to take a menstrual history than to obtain an x-ray as casually as was done here.

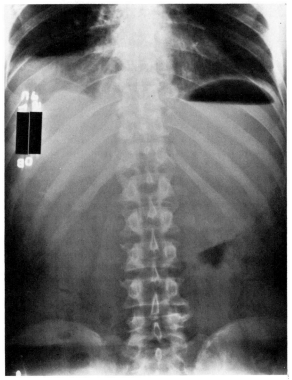

Figure 65 A   Mr. Dodge's plain film

Vomiting is **Elwood Dodge's** complaint. Elwood has been unable to keep any food down for the past 2 days. He gives you a history of gnawing indigestion, sometimes relieved by food or antacids, of two months' duration. He has lost about 10 lb. in weight over the past month. The vomitus usually consists of the food previously ingested. There has been no blood in the vomit.

Mr. Dodge is thin but does not look ill. His vital signs are normal, and his hematocrit is 39. On physical examination the only abnormality is a soft, nontender mass in the epigastrium and left upper quadrant. The bowel sounds are normal. You send Mr. Dodge to Radiology for an upper G.I. series. Figure 65A is the upright view of Mr. Dodge's abdomen. What is his problem?

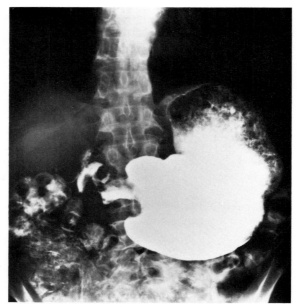

Figure 65 B   Film from the gastrointestinal series

ANSWER

The epigastric mass is the stomach, isn't it? You can see the air-fluid level in the fundus. The body of the stomach is outlined by displaced large and small intestines. Since Elwood hasn't eaten recently, the stomach must be obstructed to retain this much fluid. The two most likely causes are an obstructing duodenal or gastric ulcer, or a gastric carcinoma. His symptoms don't really lead you one way or the other.

There is no point in doing an upper G.I. series until the stomach has been emptied. Figure 65B is a 2-hour film from Elwood's gastrointestinal series obtained after 12 hours of nasogastric suction. There are still some secretions left in the stomach, but in this instance the irregular constricting lesion of the antrum is so grossly abnormal that a presumptive diagnosis of carcinoma can be made.

Elwood underwent palliative surgery, but at operation the portal lymph nodes were found to be involved with tumor.

CASE 66   VOMITING WITH SUDDEN EPIGASTRIC PAIN

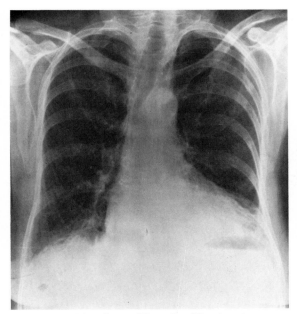

Figure 66   A   Mrs. Stuffing's chest

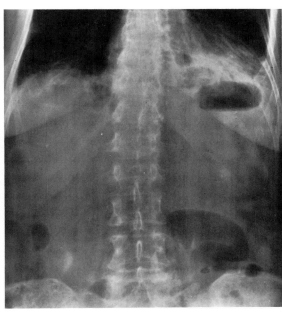

Figure 66   B   An upright film of her abdomen

Ernestine Stuffing is a 56-year-old housewife who is brought to the Emergency Room because of vomiting and chest pain. Ernestine is slightly overweight and has been on a diet. This morning, however, she suddenly gave in to her impulses and ate a box of diet cookies, four tunafish sandwiches, and a quart of ice cream with fruit topping. Following this binge she was overcome with remorse and drank a half-bottle of ipecac syrup. This induced violent vomiting.

After about 20 minutes, one especially violent episode of vomiting was accompanied by the sudden onset of midchest pain radiating through her chest to the midabdomen. The vomiting has now stopped, but the pain is getting worse and she feels very weak and frightened.

Ernestine looks ill. Her temperature is 101° (po), pulse 84, respiration 24, and blood pressure 140/88. Her EKG shows nonspecific T-wave changes. The white count is 24,900 with 75 polys, 19 bands, and 6 lymphs. Her amylase is slightly elevated. Her nasogastric aspirate is weakly guaiac-positive. Ernestine's chest is clear except for coarse rales and a pleural friction rub at the left base. Her abdomen is tense with rebound tenderness in the epigastrium. Figures 66A and B are the PA chest and upright abdominal films. Have you made the diagnosis yet?

ANSWER

The chest is normal except for bi-basilar linear densities which are seen better in the abdominal film which confirms them to be linear streaks of atelectasis or pneumonitis. The abdominal film shows more: there is a small left pleural effusion and several poorly defined pockets of air above the stomach bubble. The rest of the abdomen is grossly normal except for two loops of small bowel on the left (ileus probably). There is no free air. Do these findings support your diagnosis? How will you proceed?

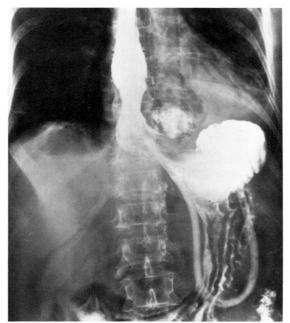

Figure 66   C   Ernestine's Gastrografin swallow

ANSWER

Figure 66C is Ernestine's Gastrografin swallow. She has a nasogastric tube in her stomach, but since you suspect an esophageal lesion, you have her swallow around the tube. The diagnosis is confirmed. Contrast leaks from a Mallory-Weiss tear in the esophagus into the mediastinum. Mrs. Stuffing was taken to the operating room, the mediastinum was drained, and the tear was repaired.

Ernestine's symptoms and signs are typical. A bout of vomiting is followed by severe crushing chest pain, usually on the left, and eventually radiating into the back. If untreated the symptoms could rapidly progress to fatal shock. The tear is usually at the posterior-lateral aspect of the esophagus.

The chest x-ray may show additional signs of mediastinal emphysema or even a pneumothorax. Free air in the abdomen is rare in *esophageal* perforations.

CASE 67 SUDDEN ESOPHAGEAL OBSTRUCTION WHILE EATING

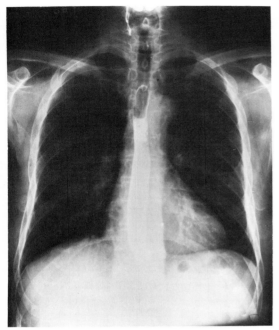

Figure 67 A Elmer Grubb's chest and esophagus

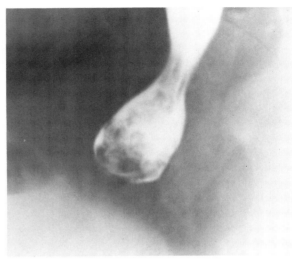

Figure 67 B The obstruction

Elmer Grubb is in town for a convention of the Fraternal Order of Muskrats. While at the opening banquet, he felt a piece of meat stick in his throat and experienced sudden lower chest pain. Drinking a large amount of water only made him vomit. Elmer tells you he has had trouble swallowing off and on for at least 5 years, but that he can usually wash food through if it sticks. He has not had any indigestion or weight loss.

Elmer's vital signs are normal and so is his physical examination. You refer him to Radiology for a barium swallow to visualize the obstruction. Figures 67A and B are the PA chest with barium and a spot film of Elmer's distal esophagus. How do you interpret them and what will you do next?

ANSWER

The chest x-ray is normal but it shows the esophagus to be obstructed and filled with barium. The esophagus is normal in caliber. The spot film of the level of obstruction shows an intraluminal filling defect which is probably the meat and which prevents you from visualizing the actual obstructing lesion. What might it be?

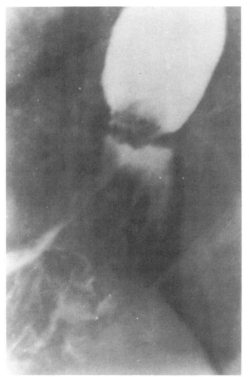

Figure 67   C   After papain

Figure 67   D   Schatzki ring

ANSWER

Well, the history of intermittent non-progressive, painless dysphagia is typical of a Schatzki ring. These benign fibrous rings are associated with hiatal hernias and do not need treatment unless the dysphagia is persistent. Ordinarily they are asymptomatic unless the diameter of the ring is less than 25 mm. The symptoms are intermittent unless the diameter is less than approximately 15 mm.

To confirm your diagnosis you must remove the meat and repeat the barium swallow. You give Elmer several tablespoons of meat tenderizer (papain) over the course of the evening, and the next morning you repeat the examination. Figures 67C and D show first the remainder of the meat caught in the ring, and then the ring alone after the meat was passed.

Elmer was discharged and is now chewing his steak more carefully. If the papain hadn't worked, the meat would have been removed at esophagoscopy.

CASE 68 A MAN WITH PROGRESSIVE DYSPHAGIA

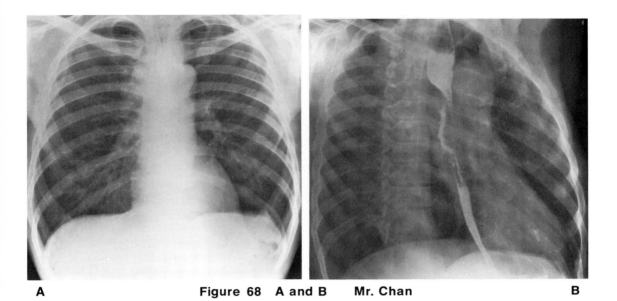

A   Figure 68 A and B   Mr. Chan   B

James Chan is a 50-year-old Chinese-American who comes to the Emergency Room at the urging of his children because he has dysphagia and has vomited up a small amount of red blood this evening. Mr. Chan is an importer who has been in good health until recently. He has had a painful sensation of fullness and dysphagia in his upper chest for about a month. He first noticed it after swallowing a very hot cup of tea, which he drinks frequently, and he thinks he "burned his throat." At dinner this evening, meat caught in his throat, and when he vomited there was a small amount of bright red blood on it.

Mr. Chan looks thin. His vital signs are normal, as is his routine lab work. On physical examination, you can palpate hard supraclavicular lymph nodes on the right. The examination is otherwise normal. Figure 68A and B are Mr. Chan's PA chest film and an oblique view from his subsequent barium swallow. What is your diagnosis?

ANSWER

The chest film is slightly abnormal. The silhouette of the right side of the superior mediastinum is usually a straight, smooth line formed by the great vessels. Here it is lobulated and irregular. The barium swallow shows a long lesion of the middle third of the esophagus with irregular collections of barium in the posterior wall. This is an ulcerating carcinoma with metastases to the medi- astinum and lymph nodes. It is an incurable lesion, unfortunately.

If patients with carcinoma present with a high-grade obstruction, they cannot be dilated with bougies. A feeding gastrostomy is necessary. Usually radiation or a bypass procedure is performed, even in incurable cases, since the unfortunate patients are made miserable by inability to swallow their oropharyngeal secretions. Mr. Chan died 3 months after coming to the Emergency Room.

SECTION XI

Obstetric Radiology

Nowhere is the art of physical examination so carefully practiced as in obstetrics. When radiographs are needed, it is usually because the physical examination is confusing or because labor is not progressing. Radiographs can demonstrate the fetal position, presentation, and attitude and can visualize or make it possible to deduce the placental position. It is therefore possible to diagnose placenta praevia, extra-uterine pregnancies, fetal death, fetal age, fetal abnormalities, and so forth. Only some of these problems fall into the area of emergency radiology.

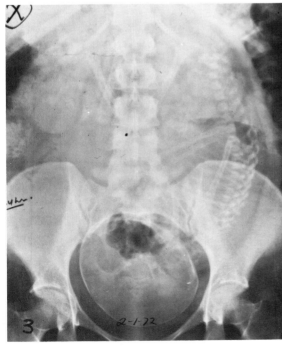

Figure 69   Baby Chadwick

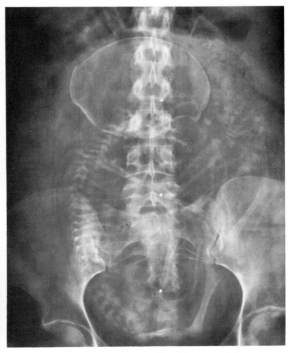

Figure 70   Baby Fernwald

Cases 69 and 70 are two healthy full-term babies. Baby Chadwick is in the vertex position. Ninety-six per cent of all babies present this way. Baby Fernwald is in a breech position with his head in the fundus of the uterus. Notice the fetal position. It has been described as one of *universal flexion*. The arms and legs are flexed and the spine is gently curved with the head flexed forward. If the baby is not in this position, beware that the fetus might be dead or that the placenta is not in its normal location. Notice also that at term the head or the rump sits low in the pelvis. The placenta is usually on the side wall, usually the anterior or the posterior side wall of the uterus.

CASE 71   THIRD TRIMESTER BLEEDING

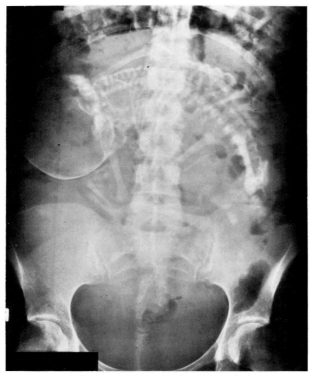

Figure 71   Baby Ladin

Mrs. Amanda Ladin, 37 weeks pregnant, is brought to the hospital by her anxious husband because she has vaginal bleeding. She has no pain and there is no history of trauma or recent sexual intercourse. Mrs Ladin is in excellent health and has had an uneventful pregnancy, though she has not seen her doctor for the past month. Examining her, you hear strong fetal heart sounds. The baby is in a transverse lie with the back in the fundus of the uterus. The bleeding, which had required 5 tampons, has stopped. What will you do next?

ANSWER

Figure 71 is a plain film of Amanda's abdomen obtained because the history and physical examination make you suspect a placenta praevia. Can you tell where the placenta is?

In general, as the fetus nears term, it assumes a position facing the placenta. That would put this baby's placenta in the pelvis or over the cervical os, a *placenta praevia.* In this instance the diagnosis is reasonably secure. A filled bladder might deceive you, and so the bladder was emptied before the x-rays were obtained. Another source of error is polyhydramnios, in which the baby is floating, as it were, in too much fluid within the uterus.

Two other methods available for making the diagnosis of placenta praevia are ultrasound or injection of a radionuclide that will localize the placenta. Ultrasound is probably the safer method and is rapidly becoming the preferred diagnostic tool.

Since Mrs. Ladin's baby is 37 weeks of age, she is taken to the operating room where the praevia is confirmed on pelvic examination. The baby was delivered by caeserean section and is doing well.

CASE 72   ABDOMINAL PAIN AND PREGNANCY

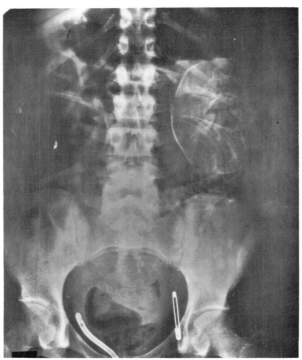

Figure 72   Baby Hegar

Emily Hegar is 8½ months pregnant. She has had a difficult pregnancy and was admitted three times in the first trimester for vomiting of pregnancy and abdominal pain. Each time she was discharged apparently in good condition, but she has continued to have abdominal pains and intermittent vomiting. Tonight she returns because of vomiting, crampy abdominal pain, and a small amount of vaginal bleeding. She says she has spotted blood for about 2 weeks. Her only other pregnancy, 6 years ago, miscarried at 3 months. She had been unable to conceive until this pregnancy.

Mrs. Hegar looks thin and tired. Her blood pressure is 118/80, pulse 100, respiration 20, and temperature 100°

(po). Her abdomen is enlarged. The bowel sounds are normal. You can palpate a fetus: the head seems to be on the left in a transverse lie. You cannot pick up fetal heart sounds or movements, but it is difficult to examine Emily because she has rebound tenderness over her upper abdomen. Her white count is 13,400 and her hematocrit is 36. Urinalysis is normal. What next?

You might do a pelvic exam, but with this history of bleeding and the transverse lie, you should worry about placenta praevia. You catheterize the bladder and obtain a film of Emily's abdomen (Fig. 72). Is this a praevia?

ANSWER

At first sight, it could be. The fetus is well above the pelvis, even for 8½ months. Notice, though, that the baby is in a high transverse lie facing *away* from the pelvis (look at the rib cage). No uterine wall can be seen separating the baby from the bowel gas. These findings suggest an extrauterine, intra-abdominal pregnancy. The baby is also in an odd position. The head is flexed right over onto the spine. This, along with the clinical examination, suggests that the fetus is not alive. Emily was taken to the operating room and a 7½ month macerated fetus was removed from the abdominal cavity.

The fetal death rate from this rare (one in 3,600 pregnancies) complication of pregnancy is 90%. The maternal death rate is about 30%, usually from hemorrhage.

CASE 73 FETAL DEATH?

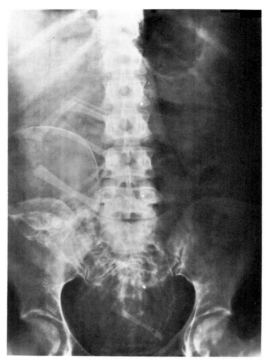

Figure 73   Baby MacDonald

Mrs. Rose MacDonald is 35 weeks pregnant. She had some first trimester bleeding but has had an uneventful pregnancy since that time. She comes to the hospital this evening because she has not felt any fetal movements all afternoon and all evening. You are unable to hear any fetal heart sounds or to feel the baby moving. Fetal death is not a life-threatening emergency for the mother, but it is a diagnosis to be made decisively. Figure 73 is Rose's abdominal film. Does it confirm your suspicions?

ANSWER

It should. The position of the fetus is abnormal. Instead of the normal position of universal flexion, the spine is in severe hyperextension, and both legs and one arm are behind the fetus. Additional signs which are not present, but may be seen about a week after fetal death, would include marked overlapping of skull bones, a halo of scalp fat elevated from the cranial vault by edema fluid, or gas in the intestines or the portal system.

CASE 74 FETAL DISTRESS: A BREECH?

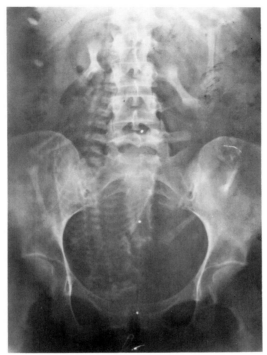

Figure 74   Baby Braxton-Hicks

Elizabeth Braxton-Hicks is a 36-year-old primipara. She has had fluid retention in the latter half of her pregnancy but has done well otherwise. She is sent to you from OB/GYN Clinic because the obstetrician examining her is having difficulty deciding whether the fetus is in vertex or breech position. When he pressed on the abdomen with the fetoscope, the fetal pulse dropped. Figure 74 is Elizabeth's KUB.

ANSWER

Sadly, this fetus is anencephalic. The easiest landmark defined, the round calvarium, is not present. Palpation of the vertex of an anencephalic (which incidentally feels like a breech) sometimes causes fetal bradycardia, probably because of pressure on the unprotected medulla. The baby was delivered at 39 weeks and died immediately after birth.

CASE 75　HYPEREMESIS GRAVIDARUM?

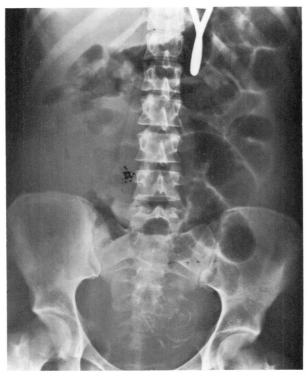

Figure 75　　Baby Roentgen

Lilly Roentgen is a 19-year-old primipara 21 weeks pregnant. She comes to the Emergency Room because of persistent vomiting. For a long time the vomiting was mild and limited to the morning and early afternoon. In the last 4 days, however, it has become almost continuous and associated with crampy abdominal pain.

Lilly's abdomen is distended, slightly more than you would expect for a 21-week gestation. Her temperature is 100°

(po), pulse 76, respiration 20, and blood pressure 116/78. Her crit is 44 and white count 9,000 with a normal differential. Examination of her abdomen reveals hyperactive and high-pitched bowel sounds. The fetal heart sounds are good. Pelvic exam confirms the fetal age, but there is the added finding of tenderness on the right. The stool is guaiac-negative as is the nasogastric aspirate. Urinalysis is normal. How will you proceed?

ANSWER

Obviously you would like to avoid radiation to the infant, even though the likelihood of radiation injury to the fetus is low. On the other hand, the physical signs suggest small intestinal obstruction or possibly appendicitis. You ask Emily if she's had her appendix out. She has, 4 years ago. You decide to get the x-ray (Fig. 75).

ANSWER

The fetus is visible in the pelvis. There are multiple loops of small bowel coiled together. They're pushed out of the pelvis by the baby and also out of the right lower quadrant. Could the right lower quadrant mass be the placenta? It could, if this is another extrauterine pregnancy.

After 6 more hours of vomiting, Lilly was exhausted and the symptoms had not abated in spite of nasogastric suction.

You and the surgeons are afraid that this is an abdominal pregnancy, with small bowel obstruction, and Lilly is taken to the Operating Room. The obstruction proved to be due to an intestinal band trapping the ileum. The pregnancy was intrauterine and (in real life) Lilly was delivered of a full-term healthy baby 4 months later.

Did the history make you think of hyperemesis gravidarum? That is what the real admission diagnosis was.

EARLY SIGNS OF PREGNANCY

Chadwick's Sign: Change in color of the cervix from pink to purplish.

Fernwald's Sign: Softening of the uterus at the site of implantation.

Hegar's Sign: Softening between the cervix and body of the uterus.

Ladin's Sign: Soft spot at the junction of the cervix and uterus.

MacDonald's Sign: Unusual ease of bringing the fundus and cervix toward each other on palpation.

Roentgen's Sign: The fetal skeleton is radiographically visible by about 16 weeks. This sign is rarely used.

SECTION XII

Ingestions and Poisonings

In general the stomach rejects poisonous materials by reflex vomiting. If it does not, the attending physician should remove the ingested material unless, as in the case of strong acids and alkalis, lavage is likely to spread the corrosive or to perforate a burned gastrointestinal tract.

In cases of ingestion, radiology is primarily useful in evaluating the lungs for evidence of aspiration or pulmonary edema, and the abdomen for evidence of perforation, ileus, peritonitis, or rarely for evidence of radiopaque poisons. In this latter category are included "tonic" pills such as iron tablets.

CASE 76 INGESTION OF ACID

Reggie Rathskeller is a connoisseur of fine wines and antique automobiles. Unfortunately, he poured the Montrachet (1959) into the battery of his Rolls Royce Silver Cloud (1923) and drank the hydrochloric acid (1 Normal) which was intended for the battery. He now comes to your Emergency Room (in the latest model ambulance) in considerable pain. He has tachycardia but is not in shock. Nevertheless, you start an IV.

His oropharynx is burned, charred in fact, and he has severe pain in his epigastrium. His bowel sounds are absent and his upper abdomen is tender to palpation. What will you do next?

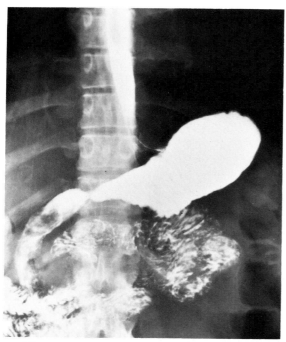

Figure 76 A   Reggie's stomach

ANSWER

You probably would do nothing more than continue intravenous fluids and begin supportive therapy, unless the chest and abdominal films showed evidence of perforation of the esophagus or bowel. In this case, however, a barium swallow was performed (Fig. 76A). It shows very poor coating of the inflamed mucosa by barium and loss of the mucosal folds in the duodenal loop which has also been burned by the acid. The stomach is *relatively* resistant to acid.

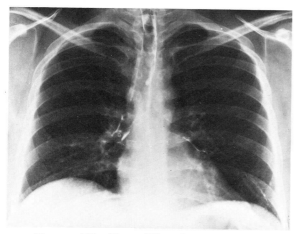

Figure 76 B   His chest film after the barium swallow

One of the main reasons you would try to *avoid* an immediate barium swallow is the danger of inducing vomiting and aspiration of acid and barium into the lungs. This is also the reason why you do not lavage patients who have ingested acid or lye. In fact, Reggie did aspirate (Fig. 76B), but only while swallowing (because of his burned pharynx). He did not vomit and aspirate. The barium will not harm his lung.

CASE 77   A CHILD WHO GOT INTO THE CLEANING CUPBOARD

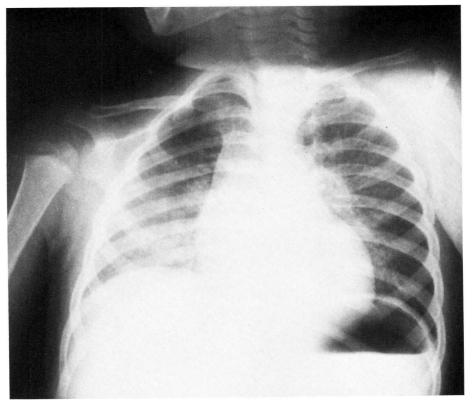

Figure 77   Ricky's chest film

Richard Rascale is a 17-month-old little boy whose mother found him alone in the kitchen surrounded by cleaning solutions. The child looked fine, but there was vomitus on the floor and he was crying. His mother called the Poison Center and was told to bring him to the Emergency Room along with the cans and bottles of solutions he might have ingested.

Richard looks well, but he smells like a cleaning establishment. The only bottle with the cap off, or even loose, contained kerosene.

A distinct aromatic odor comes from Ricky's mouth. His blood pressure and pulse are normal. However, examination of his chest is striking. He is breathing rather quickly and has moist rales throughout his chest, especially on the right. Figure 77 is his chest film. What diagnosis might you consider?

ANSWER

The film is rotated, but it is still possible to see bilateral, fairly homogeneous densities in the lung, particularly on the right. The uniformity of the density suggests a fluid, either an exudate, pneumonia, or a form of pulmonary edema. This, in fact, is "kerosene pneumonia."

We do not know whether the kerosene is aspirated during vomiting, with a resultant chemical pneumonia, or whether it is absorbed from the stomach and carried to the pulmonary capillaries, causing a chemical-induced pulmonary edema. Both mechanisms may play a part, but the known danger of aspiration is such that induction of emesis (e.g., with ipecac) is contraindicated.

The symptoms in this type of pneumonia often lag behind the x-ray, which may be abnormal within an hour or two after the kerosene has been swallowed. Unless there is superinfection, recovery is usually rapid.

Some solvents, of course, are very dangerous: benzene destroys fat-containing tissues and depresses the bone marrow; carbon tetrachloride is a liver and kidney toxin. Toxins such as these may be mixed with petroleum distillates and may initially present as a kerosene pneumonia.

CASE 78   A DEPRESSED TAX COLLECTOR

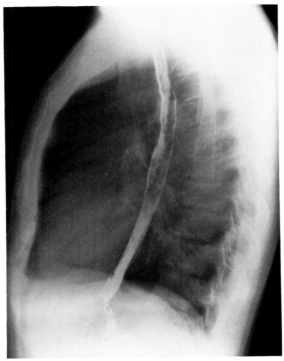

Figure 78   A   Gascoigne's initial barium swallow

Gascoigne Glum is an extremely depressed 43-year-old tax collector who is brought by the police to the Emergency Room and tells you he has drunk a mixture of Drano, whiskey, and ant poison. Strangely enough, he looks sad but not ill. You question him and he says that the mixture burned his mouth so badly that he swallowed only a sip. You are not really sure that you believe him. His physical exam seems normal, but he is complaining of pain in his throat and gullet. Looking in his mouth, there is some rather gelatinous-looking mucus, but not much else, so you send him for a careful barium swallow. Figure 78A is the lateral view, one of several films that look the same. Does it bother you?

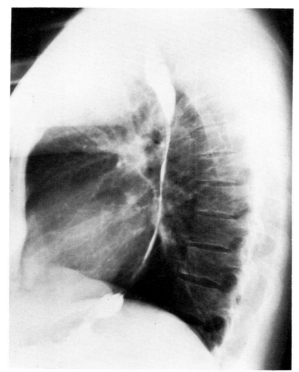

Figure 78 B   Four months later

ANSWER

It should worry you. The whole esophagus remains open without the usual stripping waves suggesting that it is atonic. The barium coats the mucosa poorly because there is too much mucus. You admit Gascoigne to the hospital.

Figure 78B is his esophagus 4 months later, showing a long stricture from the level of the aortic arch to the stomach. Ultimately, Gascoigne required an esophageal bypass operation.

Cautious esophagoscopy with a soft flexible esophagoscope would have been another approach to this problem.

SECTION XIII

Foreign Bodies

Virtually every orifice and aperture of the human body has at one time or another been found to contain a foreign body. Small children are particularly likely to insert, inhale, or swallow objects. So are the mentally unstable and the sexually inventive. Doctors and nurses account for their share of iatrogenic foreign bodies such as sponges, clamps, thermometers, enema tips, and the like.

Objects swallowed by children are the most common problem. Almost anything will pass through the alimentary tract if it can negotiate the pylorus, the bend of the duodenum, and the turn at the ligament of Treitz, and if it can pass through the terminal ileum and ileocecal valve. As a rough-and-ready rule, a foreign body longer than 2 inches is unlikely to pass the turn of the duodenum in a child less than 2 years old.

Some objects are difficult to see, among them plastics, which are a common component of modern toys. Glass is visible if it has metallic coloring or lead content. When a nonradiopaque foreign body is suspected, it may be possible to outline it by giving the patient a barium swallow.

CASE 79

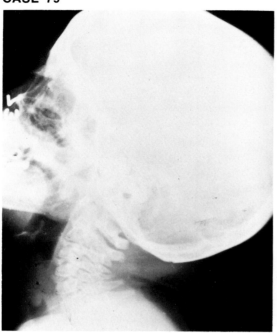

Figure 79 A Oleacea's neck

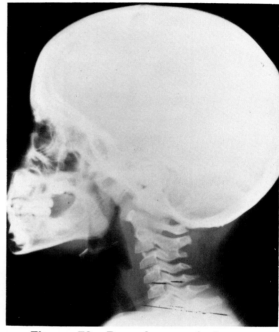

Figure 79 B A normal pharynx

Orville Oleacea and **Studds Oligophagus** are two difficult children who rarely eat what is set before them. This evening, however, they are brought to the Emergency Room by their mothers because they have eaten what was not set before them, and they are now choking and coughing. Figures 79A and 80A and B are the neck films obtained on Orville and Studds. (Figure 79B is a post-treatment normal film for comparison.) Which child is more likely to get into trouble?

ANSWER

Obviously it is much more dangerous to have a foreign body in the trachea than in the esophagus. Look at the air column of **Orville's** upper trachea. That convex density is the bottom of an olive pit (*Oleacea*-olive tree) lodged just below the vocal cords. Orville is lucky to be alive. The olive pit does not completely obstruct the trachea and allows the passage of some air. It was successfully removed at bronchoscopy.

Where do you suppose aspirated foreign bodies usually lodge? At the narrow points—the vocal cords and the larynx—or at the tracheal bifurcation. From this, it follows that, in an emergency, the foreign body should either be within reach of the fingers or forceps at the level of the vocal cords or at the tracheal bifurcation, in which case a tracheostomy will be of no use.

CASE 80

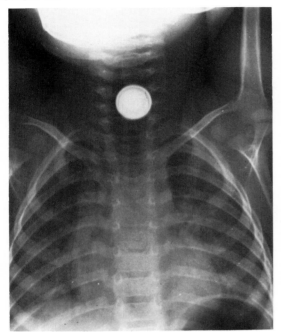

A

Figure 80   A and B   Studds' neck films   B

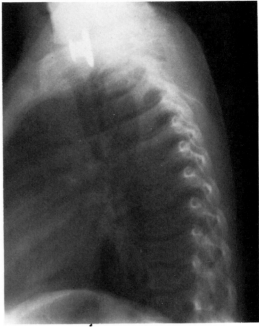

Now, what about **Studds?** That is a collar stud. It is oriented in a coronal plane, typical of a foreign body within the esophagus. Foreign bodies of this general shape, coins for example, lodge in a coronal plane in the esophagus and in a sagittal plane in the trachea. This orientation is probably due to the fact that the posterior wall of the trachea has no cartilage and is the only direction in which the tracheal lumen can be stretched. This orientation, incidentally, is not an academic point. A foreign body lodged in the esophagus very commonly presses on the trachea and causes the child to have spells of coughing, making the observer suspect a tracheal foreign body.

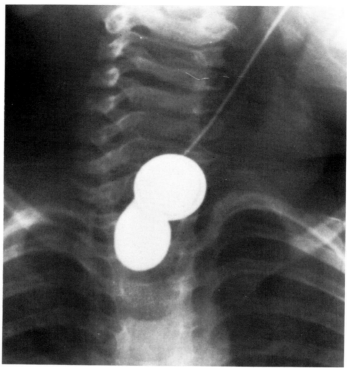

Figure 80 C   How to remove a foreign body from the upper esophagus

It was a simple matter to remove young Studds' collar button. A Foley balloon was passed down the esophagus (Fig. 80C) past the offending button, inflated with radiopaque contrast material so that it could be seen, and then gently pulled back, bringing the stud with it.

CASES 81, 82, AND 83   THREE SWALLOWED FOREIGN BODIES

Here are three more omniverous children brought to see you because of their eating habits. Figures 81, 82 and 83 are their plain films. What have they swallowed, and which child is likely to get into trouble?

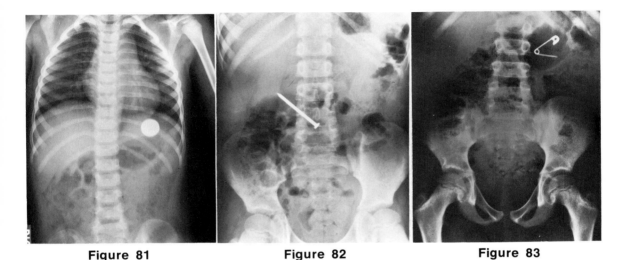

Figure 81   Figure 82   Figure 83

ANSWER

The objects are a coin, a nail, and an open (diaper) pin.

The coin, a quarter, should present no problem at all and doesn't need to be followed, since you can have the mother examine the stools. This will serve as an additional reminder to the mother that more dangerous objects may be swallowed.

The nail is more likely to be a problem, since it is long and may have difficulty negotiating the duodenum and the turn at the ligament of Treitz.

The open safety pin is the most worrisome object, since it may easily lodge in the bowel and perforate the bowel wall. It should be followed with serial x-rays, probably every 3 or 4 hours at first and then daily until it is passed. If its progress ceases for more than a day, or if the child develops abdominal pain, you must consider the possibility that the pin has become lodged or has perforated the bowel. Operation may then be necessary.

In actual fact, all three objects made an uneventful journey through the gastrointestinal tract.

CASES 84 AND 85 TWO FOREIGN OBJECTS INSERTED FROM BELOW

Children are not the only ones who place foreign materials in orifices. Children will put anything anywhere; adults seem to have a predilection for inserting things in the rectum and genitourinary tract. The motive seems usually to be sexual stimulation, but accidents and desperate attempts to relieve constipation have their place. Figures 84 and 85 are two adults, neither of whom would volunteer a history. Can you deduce what has taken place?

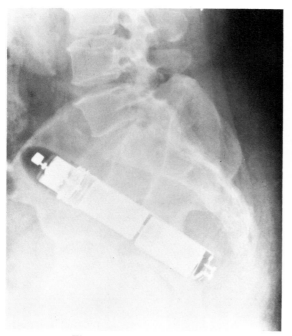

Figure 84   A UFO?

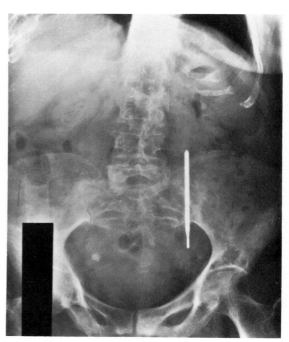

Figure 85   Is it in the colon?

ANSWER

Figure 84 is a lateral view of the rectum and pelvis. The rocket ship–like device with batteries on the small electric motor is a "vibrator" high in the rectum. Proctoscopic attempts at removal failed, and sigmoidotomy was finally necessary for its removal.

Is that thermometer (Fig. 85) in this elderly lady's sigmoid? It could be: thermometers are often found incidentally on abdominal x-rays. In this case, however, the thermometer was in the bedclothes, and there are three clues to that fact on the film: (1) This is an oral thermometer, not a rectal thermometer (look at the shape of the bulb). (2) The bulb is directed outward not inward. (3) The thermometer is not broken, as is often the case if it has been inserted much beyond the rectum.

CASES 86, 87, AND 88 FOREIGN BODIES IN THE HANDS AND FEET

Hands and feet are common locations for foreign material. If there is a complex injury, a fracture may distract the observer from foreign bodies such as metal, glass, gravel, etc., any of which commonly contaminate open wounds. Can you tell what the objects are in Figures 86, 87, and 88?

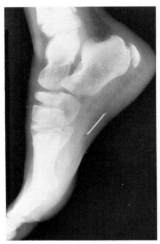

Figure 86

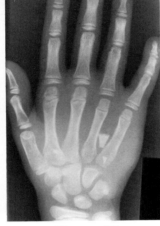

Figure 87

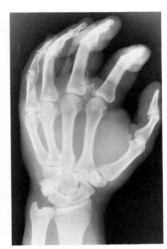

Figure 88

ANSWER

Let's start with the foot (Fig. 86). The long, thin metallic object is a sewing needle. Did you notice that there is a second fragment missing from the eye of the needle and that it is located under the metatarsals?

Figure 87 is a child's hand (look at the epiphyses). In it there is a sharply geometric, faintly radiodense foreign body. This is the typical appearance of window glass (jammed into the palm of the hand as the little girl fell onto a storm window).

The adult hand (Fig. 88) contains fine radiating strands or spicules of radiodense material at the base of the 3rd finger. This is lead paint accidentally injected into the palm of the hand by a workman holding a paint spray gun.

The needle and the glass were removed without difficulty. The painter, however, developed a severe cellulitis which spread into the fascial planes of the hand and ultimately had to be drained surgically.

CASES 89, 90, AND 91 THREE PATIENTS WITH GAS IN THE SOFT TISSUES

Gas in the soft tissues may be normal, as in the case of an acute open laceration. Gas in a wound which has been closed implies a serious wound infection.

Figures 89, 90A and B, and 91 are three patients with gas in the soft tissues. Can you reconstruct their stories?

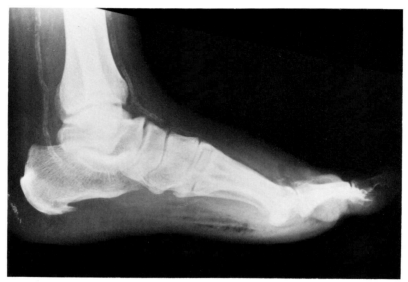

Figure 89

ANSWER

Figure 89 is a 56-year-old diabetic with a Proteus cellulitis of the sole of his foot. Dense calcification of the pedal vessels is rare except in diabetics. The combination of small vessel disease and peripheral neuropathy makes diabetics particularly prone to foot infections which they underestimate or neglect. In this case the whole story can be deduced from the x-rays.

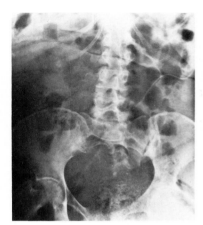 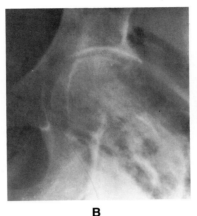 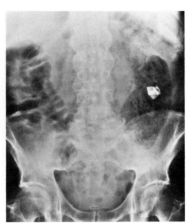

A Figure 90   A and B   Plain film and blowup of left hip   Figure 91   A post-op fever

Figures 90A and B are much more difficult to explain from the plain film alone. The blowup shows you a magnified view of the left hip. This is an elderly lady from a nursing home referred because of multiple bedsores on her back. But look at the blowup of the left hip. That is gas in the muscle planes about the hip. The insinuation of gas into the (necrotic) muscle is characteristic of a Clostridium infection. The extent of the infection had not been recognized clinically and was picked up only incidentally on the abdominal film.

The last abdominal film (Fig. 91) is a classic. This patient began to run a fever one day following abdominal surgery. By the third postoperative day he had fevers, chills, sweats, *E. coli* in the blood, and a flank mass. That ribbon-like radiodensity is a marker on a sponge inadvertently left in the abdomen. The bubbly lucencies around it are gas in a large retroperitoneal abscess. He was re-explored, the sponge was removed, and the abscess was drained. He recovered without further complications.

CASES 92 AND 93 MORE PATIENTS WITH RADIODENSE
FOREIGN BODIES

Can you deduce the nature of these foreign bodies (Figs. 92 and 93A and B)?

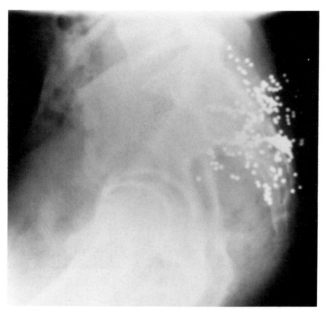

Figure 92   A lateral "shot" of buttocks

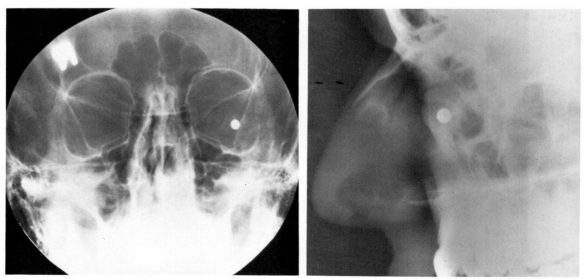

Figure 93   A and B   AP and lateral views of orbit

ANSWER

It's not hard, really. Figure 92, a lateral view, is the backside of a traveling salesman who was clearly on the wrong end of a Farmer's Daughter joke. This is buckshot scattered about his gluteal muscles. He is, in fact, that famous ladies' man, Robin "Breezy" Belaire, of *Exercises* Volume 2, page 58.

Figures 92A and B, frontal and lateral views of the face and orbit, show a more serious problem. That is a BB pellet in the eye. The lateral view shows it to be far anterior, just beneath the soft tissues of the eyelids (arrow). It proved it to be embedded in the (bloody) sclera but did not perforate the globe; BB pellets from air guns usually do not perforate the eye.

If the foreign body had been intraocular, several methods of localization would have been available. Visual inspection with an ophthalmoscope is the best method but is not always feasible, especially if there is blood in the vitreous. Since the size of the globe corresponds roughly to a quarter, an estimate of the position of a foreign body can be made with that rule in mind. If the object is then thought to be intraocular, its position relative to the central axis (of motion) of the globe may be deduced by obtaining radiographs with the patient looking up and down or from side to side. The Sweet method of localization is a precise variant of this method in which the intraocular position is transcribed from the x-ray to calibrated graph paper.

Usually *exact* localization by radiography is not necessary unless the object is retro-orbital or lies near a vital structure such as the optic nerve.

CASES 94 AND 95 TWO BIZARRE PATIENTS

Believe it or not, both these patients walked into the hospital. **Steven Blue** (Fig. 94) has a towel on his head and looks sad. **Elvira High** is a nurse in your hospital who comes to the Emergency Room because of a chest cold (Fig. 95A and B).

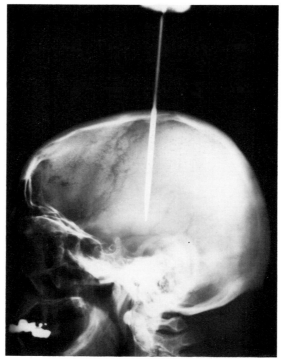

Figure 94   Mr. Blue

ANSWER

Mr. Blue is suicidal. He first tried to kill himself with a hatchet, and finally hammered an ice pick into his skull. Had he hammered it a little further, he would have impaled the midbrain and succeeded in his suicidal attempt.

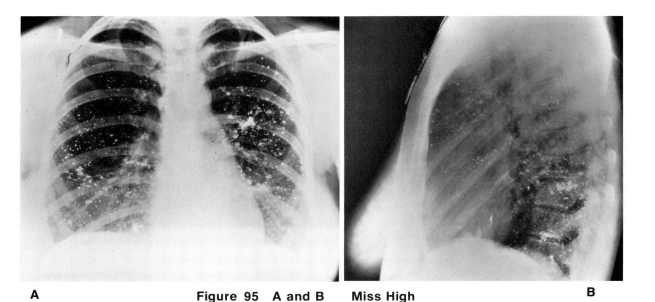

A   **Figure 95 A and B   Miss High**   **B**

Nurse High has many metallic densities in her chest. They must be in the chest, not on it, since the soft tissues are normal and the densities project over only the lungs in both views. Nurse High had been mainlining mercury from thermometers for several months. The densities are elemental mercury in her pulmonary arteries. It is not known what effect the mercury had on her mood. She was unstable anyway.

SECTION XIV

Fractures

In the preceding sections of this volume we have arranged our cases according to chief complaint and have provided as much clinical information as was, or could be expected to be, available. In this section dealing with fractures we will vary the format slightly.

Clinical signs of fractures include swelling, bruising, deformity, bone pain or tenderness, loss of motion, audible crepitus with motion, and abnormal motion. These symptoms and signs have sufficed for diagnosis and reasonably successful treatment of fractures for centuries. However, the additional use of radiographs has speeded and refined treatment to the degree that excellent results are the rule and complications the exception. In fact, the radiologic examination has become an integral part of the examination of suspected fractures. Radiographs are a medicolegal necessity in many instances, as well as a clinical necessity, and almost no fracture is set without a previous x-ray. As a result, the initial examination of the injured part is brief and manipulation is avoided until the radiographs have been obtained.

The clinical information given to the radiologist in cases of suspected fracture is likely to be something like "Fell on outstretched hand. Rule out fracture." Brief as it is, this laconic version of the patient's complaint is very useful, since most fractures can be predicted if the mechanism of injury is known.

In this section we will show you some common injuries along with the brief history and complaint which would be available to you at the time the radiographs were obtained. To save space we have not always shown you all the x-rays which were obtained. Remember, though, that several views are usually needed and that at least two views are needed in any displaced fracture. As in the other sections, the important details in all the cases are factual.

CASES 96, 97, 98, 99, and 100 PAIN IN THE WRIST. FELL ON OUTSTRETCHED HAND

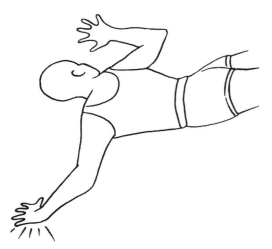

The Magnificent Credenzas are a famous family of acrobats who perform balancing feats on a tightrope. While practicing a pyramid act in which they were all balanced on the shoulders of one man, the wire broke and they fell 5 feet to the ground landing on their outstretched hands. They are brought to your Emergency Room with wrist pain. You are presented with the family: **Manicotti,** age 34, **Straticelli,** age 70, **Lasagne,** age 11, **Zucchini,** age 22, and **Zabaglioni,** age 24. Can you diagnose their fractures?

Figure 96 A The fall

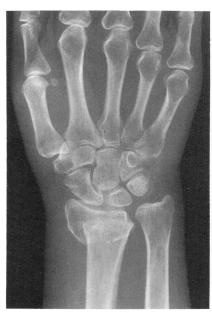 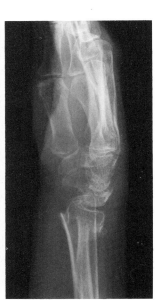

Figure 96 B and C Manicotti

ANSWER

The Credenzas have all sustained hyperextension injuries of the wrist which have resulted from a fall on a dorsiflexed, pronated hand (Fig. 96A). When the hand struck the ground, twisting, flexing, and compressing forces were transmitted by the carpals to the distal radius.

In adults (**Manicotti,** Fig. 96B and C), if there is a fracture, it is usually through the distal radius within one inch of the wrist, with dorsal, and often radial, angulation of the distal fragment. This is a so-called Colles' fracture. In older patients (**Straticelli,** Fig. 97A and B) with weaker and more brittle bones, the distal fragment is likely to be comminuted, the ulnar tip may also fracture, and, in general, the dorsal displacement and overriding of the fracture fragments is greater, as is the case here.

The bones of children are much more flexible, and a "greenstick" or "torus" fracture (**Lasagne,** Fig. 98A and B) of the distal radius is likely to occur. This fracture is visible on the lateral film as a buckling of the cortex (arrow) of the dorsal aspect of the distal radius.

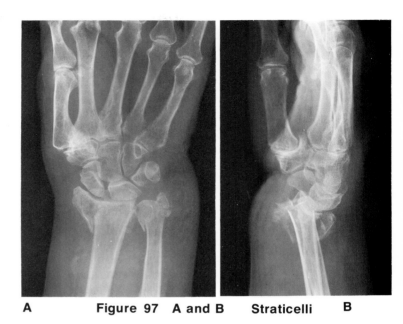

A   Figure 97   **A and B**   **Straticelli**   **B**

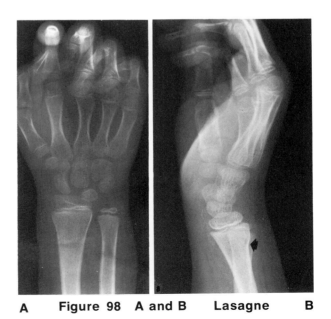

A   Figure 98   **A and B**   **Lasagne**   **B**

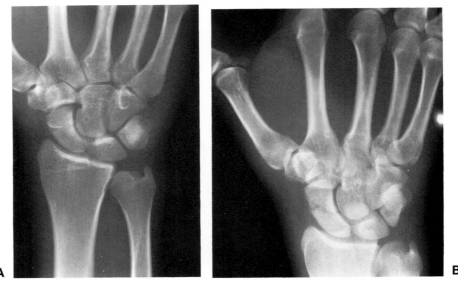

Figure 99   A and B   Zucchini

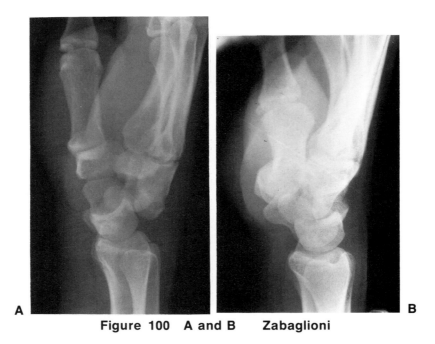

Figure 100   A and B   Zabaglioni

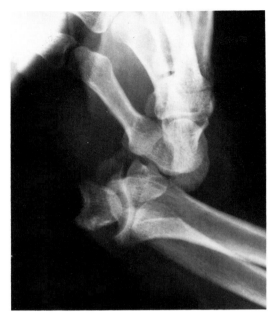

Figure 100 C   **Perilunate dislocation**

The carpal bones of the wrist are held in a relatively fixed position by their articulations with one another and by connecting ligaments. The navicular bone acts as a strut between the proximal row of carpals and the distal row. If the apex of the flexing forces is at the level of the carpals, instead of at the level of the distal radius, the navicular may be fractured by bending forces. This fracture is clinically manifest by point tenderness at the base of the thumb in the "anatomic snuffbox." Radiographically this is a difficult fracture to see unless the hand is positioned carefully. This injury is most common in young men. **Zucchini** (Fig. 99A and B) has suffered a fracture of his navicular, visible only on the oblique film (Fig. 99B).

Once the navicular strut is broken, the carpus can bend, and, if hyperextended far enough, the proximal row of carpals can dislocate from the distal row. This usually occurs at the level of the capitate-lunate articulation. **Zabaglioni's** lunate has popped forward. (The lunate is the half-moon-shaped bone which articulates with the end of the radius.) Figures 100A and B show his dislocation and the normal postreduction film. Figure 100C is a different patient in whom the lunate has remained aligned with the radius, but the rest of the carpus has dislocated posteriorly. These two fractures are known as lunate and perilunate dislocations, respectively.

CASES 101, 102, AND 103   THREE MORE PATIENTS WHO FELL ON OUTSTRETCHED HANDS

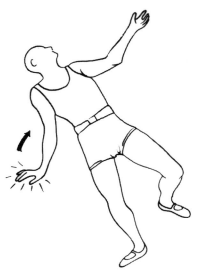

Figure 101   A   The fall

Shortly after the Credenza family has been treated, you are astonished to be confronted by a second circus family, **The Olympus Tumblers. Aristophanes, Archimedes,** and their young brother **Euripides** have all fallen backwards while practicing a new "collapsing tower" routine. They have broken their fall by reaching behind them with outstretched hands (Fig. 101A).

The basic mechanism of these three injuries is forced flexion and supination of the wrist or forearm. The majority of the forces come into play when the hand hits the ground and is fixed, and the body continues to fall and twist. Can you identify the fractures?

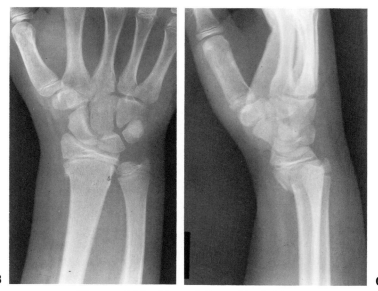

B   C

Figure 101   B and C   Euripides

ANSWER

Euripides (Fig. 101B and C) has a "Smith's" or reverse Colles' fracture with palmar angulation of the distal radial fragment. This fracture may also be sustained by falling forward onto the back of a flexed hand and wrist.

Archimedes (Fig. 102A and B) has a more serious injury with marked palmar displacement of the distal radial fragment and dislocation at the distal radio-ulnar joint. This dislocation, the result of hypersupination at the wrist, is apt to be disabling if it is not corrected at surgery. Open reduction is necessary to restore the integrity of avulsed ligaments.

Aristophanes (Fig. 103) has a less serious and more common injury, a fracture-dislocation of the base of the thumb—"Bennett's fracture." Notice that this is a fracture-*dislocation;* there is a fracture through the base of the first metacarpal with dislocation of the radial portion of the articular surface, while the smaller medial fragment remains in normal relationship to the carpal trapezium.

Even though this is a relatively simple fracture, it should not be underestimated. The thumb is functionally one of the most important joints in the body. Adequate reduction and immobilization is necessary to restore function and to prevent secondary osteoarthritic changes which could be disabling in some occupations.

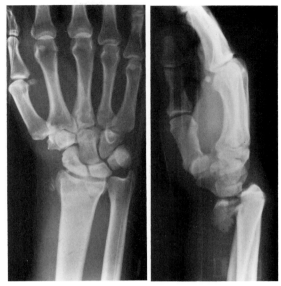

A Figure 102 A and B Archimedes B

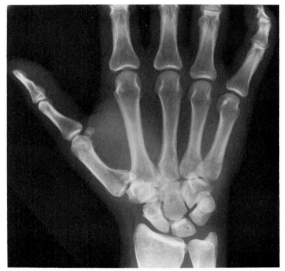

Figure 103 Aristophanes

CASES 104, 105, 106, AND 107   FELL ON OUTSTRETCHED ARM

These four men are members of an amateur rowing club. They were carrying their brand-new Crowley-Lambordi shell from the boathouse when the Stroke slipped and began to fall. The herculean efforts of the crew to protect the fragile shell were successful: they kept it balanced on their right shoulders while they fell sideways, breaking the fall with their outstretched arms (Fig. 104A).

The mechanism of these fractures is this: the patient falls on his outstretched arm, the acromion locks against the humerus and acts as a fulcrum at the base of the greater tuberosity, making the humerus become the long arm of a lever. The humeral head may dislocate anteriorly. If it does not, the effect of the fall is forced abduction of the humerus. The common resultant fracture is avulsion of the greater tuberosity or a fracture through the cervical neck of the humerus. In old patients with brittle bones, the fracture may be comminuted. Which oarsman has sustained which injury?

Figure 104   A   The fall

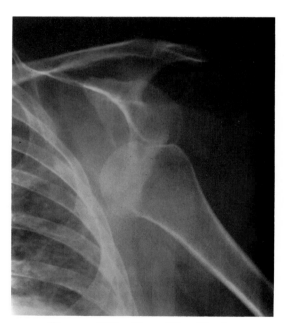

Figure 104   B   The Stroke

ANSWER

Archibald, the Stroke (Fig. 104B), has sustained an anterior dislocation. The humeral head is displaced anteriorly and inferiorly and rests on the (inferior) rim of the glenoid fossa of the scapula. Neither the glenoid nor the humerus is fractured in this case, but they often are.

Brewster, Number 3 Oar (Fig. 105), has not dislocated his shoulder, but he has avulsed his greater tuberosity. Luckily, the fracture fragment remains in roughly anatomic position and surgery is not necessary. If the fragment had retracted into the joint space or retracted far enough to make the abductor muscles of the shoulder lax, then open (surgical) reduction and fixation would have been necessary.

Chester, the Number 2 man in the boat (Fig. 106), has suffered an impacted fracture of the surgical neck of the humerus. The fracture is comminuted, but remains in anatomic alignment. He does not need surgery.

Dunster, the Bow Oar (Fig. 107), did not have time to put his arm out. He fell on the tip of his shoulder. The acromion protected the shoulder joint, but he has ruptured the acromioclavicular ligament and has an acromioclavicular separation. As was the case here, this injury usually results from direct trauma to the shoulder tip.

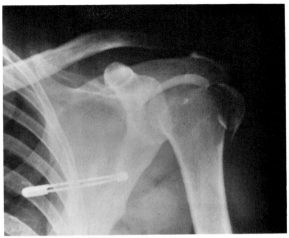

Figure 105   The Number 3 "Oar"

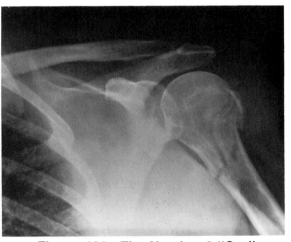

Figure 106   The Number 2 "Oar"

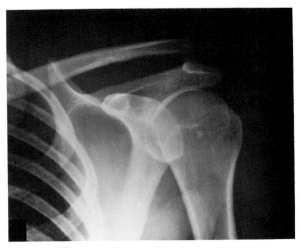

Figure 107   The Bow "Oar"

CASES 108, 109, AND 110   TWISTED ANKLE

Injuries to the ankle joint are almost as common as injuries to the hand and wrist. They are the most common injuries of athletes and are usually the result of forced inversion of the foot. The foot may be forcibly inverted in a fall, or it may be fixed (as by the cleats on athletic shoes) while the body falls and twists. The next three patients are all competitors at an international track meet.

Alonzo Vaporelli (Fig. 108), a hurdler for Italy, caught his left foot on the high hurdles and came crashing down on his right foot.

Hans Henke (Fig. 109A and B), a German shot-putter, swung around to begin his spin and felt a sudden pain in his right ankle, which is now swollen. His foot hurts when he walks.

Sonny Henderson (Fig. 110A and B) is a pole-vaulter from UCLA competing for the United States. He cleared the bar but missed the landing pit, and now has a swollen, painful ankle which he thinks is fractured.

All three competitors have sustained severe forced inversion injuries. Less forcible inversion would probably tear some fibers of the collateral ligaments of the ankle (a sprain). Here the ligaments have held, and the bones have fractured. Can you identify these fractures?

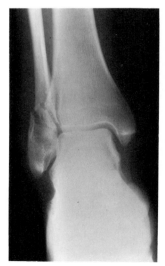
Figure 108   Alonzo

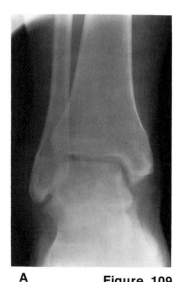
A

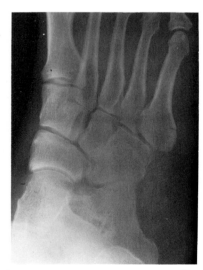
B

Figure 109   A and B   Hans

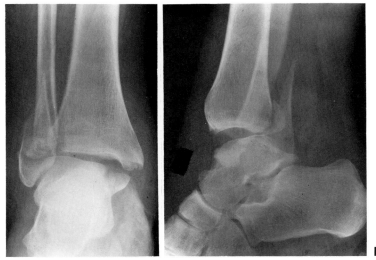

Figure 110   A and B   Sonny

ANSWER

Alonzo has a fracture of his distal fibula. The diagonal, spiral course of the fracture reflects the twisting forces of inversion injuries. The fracture is still in anatomic alignment, with the distal fibula up against the talus. The ankle "mortise" is thus preserved, and the ankle joint will be stable if the fracture is put in a cast in this position.

Hans has a swollen ankle. The fracture, however, is not in his ankle; it is at the base of the 5th metatarsal. The wind-up for the shot-put twisted the foot into forced inversion and plantar flexion, spraining the collateral ligament. In addition, the base of the 5th metatarsal has been pulled off by the tendon of the peroneus brevis. These are commonly associated injuries. As is the case here, there is rarely any significant displacement of this fracture. Hans' sprained ankle and fractured foot were put in a cast.

Sonny's injury is the most serious. Again, the force is inversion (internal rotation and plantar flexion), but the force was more violent than in the previous two cases. As the foot inverted in relation to the leg, the lateral malleolus was sheared off and the ankle mortise opened, allowing the talus to snap off first the medial malleolus of the tibia and then the posterior lip (or malleolus) of the tibia.

The medial and lateral malleolar fractures are visible on the AP view. The posterior lip fracture is seen on the lateral view. The ankle mortise is now lost, and the foot is dislocated posteriorly. This fracture had to be reduced surgically because of the extent of the injury and because the small malleolar fragments are more likely to heal if fixed in place by screws.

The ankle joint is extremely important in function. It is constantly bearing weight. If the ankle mortise is not returned to proper alignment, disabling arthritis will result. Remember, too, that the ankle may need casting for a bad sprain. If the ligaments are seriously stretched or heal with laxity, the ankle will be unstable. This, too, is likely to result in degenerative arthritis.

CASES 111 AND 112 TWO SKIERS WITH BROKEN LEGS

You manage to find yourself a *locum tenens* in Ski Country with the mornings to ski and the afternoons to work in a nearby Emergency Room. Your first day is busy. **"Crash" Kelly** (Fig. 111) is a slalom racer who caught the tip of his ski on a slalom pole, crossed his skis, and lived up to his name as he spiraled into the edge of the course. **"Hot Dog" Barnes** (Fig. 112) is a downhill racer who failed to unweight on a mogul and caught his right ski in a rut. "Hot Dog" hurtled forward, but his boots did not come out of the bindings. What do you make of these fractures?

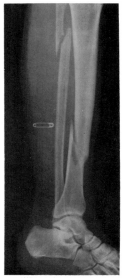

Figure 111   "Crash" Kelly

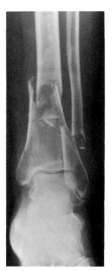

Figure 112   "Hot Dog" Barnes

ANSWER

These are two common ski injuries. **"Crash"** twisted his leg until the tibia and then the fibula sustained spiral fractures. He was treated by closed reduction. **"Hot Dog"** has a more difficult injury to treat. When the heel of his ski boot failed to release from the binding, the forward momentum of his body snapped both tibia and fibula at the boot top. These boot-top fractures have become more common with the introduction of high boots made of inflexible plastics. This fracture is extremely unstable because there is a relatively small surface area for bone apposition. It was reduced surgically and an intramedullary rod was placed in the tibia. Both skiers have returned to the racing circuit.

SECTION XV

Injuries to the Spine

The spine is intrinsically unstable, being composed of a column of blocks which are interlocked by facets and attached by ligaments, to be sure, but which are mainly stabilized and protected by the muscles of the neck, chest, and trunk. The thoracic spine is relatively resistant to injury, probably because of the added support of the rib cage. Injuries to the lumbar spine are more common. This is mainly because of its anatomic instability and the lack of muscle tone which most of us experience as we grow older; the abdominal musculature becomes flabby and lumbar lordosis increases.

In back injuries the "trauma" is often trivial. Lifting a heavy book from a high shelf or pulling a briefcase out of the back seat of a car may stretch one or more of the many stabilizing muscles of the spine beyond its normal limits. The muscle then goes into spasm which puts abnormal stress on other muscles, and a vicious circle is set up. The pain may be intense. More serious trauma may rupture ligaments and fracture vertebrae, but the majority of patients coming to the Emergency Room with back pain have primarily muscular injuries. Since muscle spasm usually accompanies fractures, it may be difficult to exclude a fracture or bone lesions without an x-ray. On the other hand, consider the fact that many patients with low back pain are men in the reproductive age. The radiation dose of lumbar spine films is small but is aimed at the gonads. Deciding whether or not a patient really needs an x-ray can therefore be a problem.

The cervical spine is not ordinarily subjected to undue stresses and strains in the course of daily activities. However, automobile accidents, even minor ones, may subject the cervical spine to sudden hyperflexion, often followed by hyperextension, the combination injury being termed "whiplash." Since car accidents are common, we see a lot of patients with whiplash injuries. As in the lumbar spine, the muscular injuries of whiplash may be exquisitely painful even when there is no fracture present.

Andrew Argyle (Fig. 113A, B, and C), **Benegino Barbaroli** (Fig. 114A and B), and **Christos Christopoulos** (Fig. 115A and B) are three young men who work for Transcontinental Movers. While trying to maneuver a grand piano up a spiral staircase, they lost their footing and almost lost the piano. All three are sent by their foreman to "get x-rays."

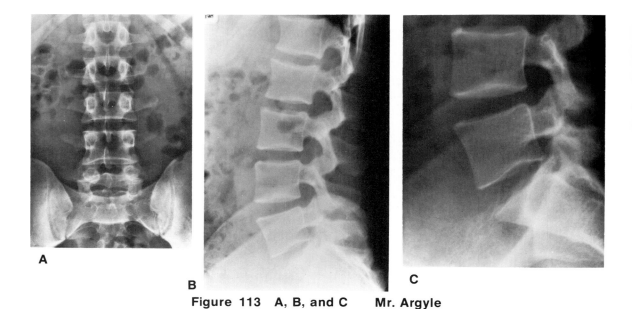

A

B

C

Figure 113   A, B, and C   Mr. Argyle

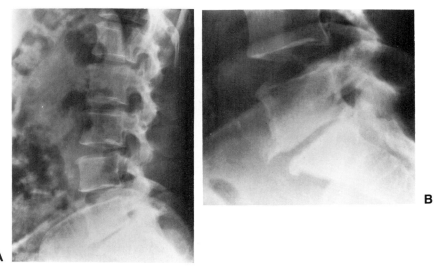

A

B

Figure 114   A and B   Mr. Barbaroli

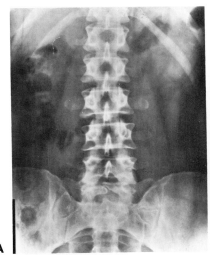
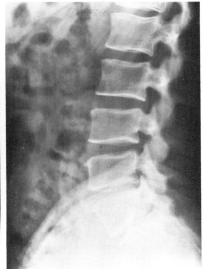

Figure 115   A and B   Mr. Christopoulos

ANSWER

They have one radiologic finding in common—narrowing of the L5–S1 intervertebral space. In general, the height of the lumbar interspaces increases progressively down the spine. You might therefore think that these men are suffering from crushed or "slipped" intervertebral discs; they are not.

Andrew's spine is normal. The rule of increasing interspace width does not hold true for the L5–S1 level, which is often slightly narrower than L4–5. Andrew's lordosis is normal. There is no sclerosis of the vertebral end plates, and the bones are intact.

What about **Benegino?** Well, there is considerable narrowing at the L5–S1 level, with dense sclerosis of the apposed surfaces and with marginal osteophytes; this is certainly not normal. It is true that the disc must be flattened in this case, but that amount of sclerosis and spurring tell you that this is not an acute injury.

Christos? The last two interspaces are narrower than the ones above. This could be a pathologic finding, but the AP view shows you that the lowest vertebra is not completely incorporated into the sacrum and has large transverse processes which articulate with the sacrum on the left. This is a so-called transitional vertebra. Anatomically it may be considered part of the sacrum. Its disc space is normally quite narrow, and the interspace above it is usually considered to be L5–S1. (There is also an incidental finding of a spina bifida occulta of the transitional vertebra.)

None of these young men had back pain, spasm, or nerve irritation on straight leg-raising at the time of examination. They did not need x-rays. You send them out but warn them to expect some backache tomorrow.

CASES 116, 117, 118, 119, 120, AND 121
AN AUTOMOBILE COLLISION WITH NECK INJURIES

The following six patients were riding in a limousine together on their way to the annual picnic of Mensa, an organization composed of individuals with IQ's over 160. One of them was entertaining the others with the following problem:

You have eight weights, one of which is heavier than the others, and a balance scale which you can use only twice. How would you find the odd weight?

Unfortunately, the driver (IQ = 120) became so engrossed in this problem that he ran smack into the back of a parked truck. The clever occupants were not smart enough to be wearing shoulder belts and are now brought to you with what is thought to be whiplash injuries.

The driver was thrown through the windshield and also has neck pain. As a preliminary step, you obtain AP and lateral views of the neck without moving the patients from their stretchers in case they have unstable fractures of the spine. (Only the pertinent views are shown.)

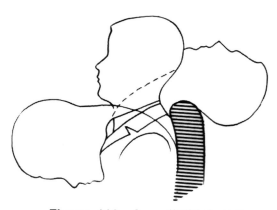

Figure 116 A   "Whiplash"

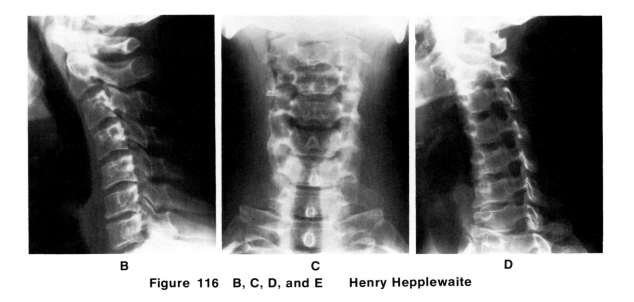

B   C   D

Figure 116   B, C, D, and E   Henry Hepplewaite

ANSWER

Henry Hepplewaite (Fig. 116B to E) has no visible fractures or dislocation on the AP and lateral views, so you obtain flexion and extension and oblique views. There is no subluxation, but all the views show a marked reversal of the normal dorsal lordosis. This is the result of the hyperextension component of the hyperflexion-hyperextension (whiplash) injury (Fig. 116A). The snapback of the head over the back of the automobile seat stretches the anterior muscles of the neck far beyond their normal limit, and they go into spasm causing the abnormal curvature of the spine. The "whiplash injury" may be composed only of muscle contusions and hemorrhages but it may be accompanied by similar stretch injuries of the ligaments and nerve roots.

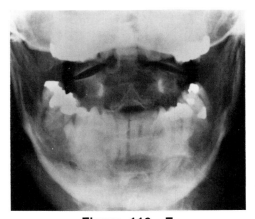

Figure 116   E

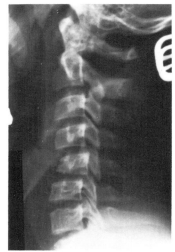

Figure 117   Isidore Inchfinger

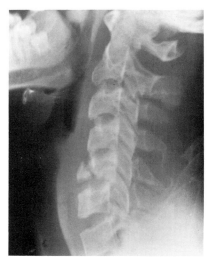

Figure 118 A   John Jackstone

WHIPLASH INJURIES

Isadore Inchfinger (Fig. 117), the 16-year-old virtuoso intellect of the group, has neck pain but no neurologic deficit. He has sustained an anterior wedge fracture of C5. The fractured vertebra is slightly posterior to the rest of the spine but proved to be stable. There were no other fractures, and Isadore recovered uneventfully. The wedge fracture is caused by the flexion component of the whiplash.

John Jackstone (Fig. 118A) was not so lucky. He was brought in with a central cord syndrome (asymmetric paresis and sensory loss in his upper and lower extremities). His spine is normally aligned now, but there is evidence of a severe hyperflexion-hyperextension injury. In addition to a wedge fracture of C5, a fragment of bone has been avulsed from the inferior aspect of C5. When the spine was hyperextended, the anterior longitudinal ligament of the spine ruptured (note the soft tissue swelling) and tore off the telltale fragment from the bottom of C5. The same severe hyperextension caused the ligamentum flavum on the posterior wall of the spinal canal to bulge inward, compressing the cord (Fig. 118B).

Even tiny anterior "teardrop" fractures from the anterior surface of nearby vertebrae should be regarded with caution, since central cord syndrome which is due to hemorrhage and edema may be delayed in onset, and may also be exacerbated by needless neck motion, even in the absence of an unstable spine.

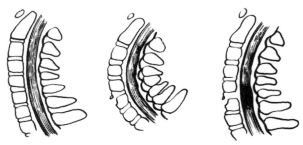

Figure 118 B   Mechanism of central cord compression

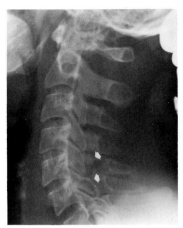

Figure 119
Kermit Knapflugle

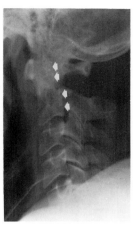

Figure 120
Lewis Lurchpast

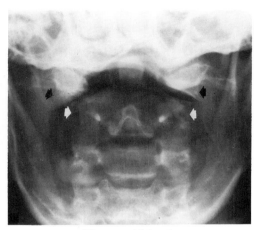

Figure 121 A
Marvin Masterstroke

Kermit Knapflugle (Fig. 119) has no neurologic deficit, but he is in danger of developing one. His whiplash has avulsed the spinous processes of C4 and C5 and the laminae of C5. His spine is now unstable and must be carefully supported until surgery is performed.

Incidentally, even if you can't tell what fracture has occurred (because of film technique or because of inexperience), it is wise to consider all fractures involving the posterior elements of the spine as unstable until shown otherwise.

Lewis Lurchpast (Fig. 120) also has a potentially serious injury. Look at the back of his odontoid. It should be exactly aligned with the back of C2 (arrows) from which it extends (compare with Fig. 119). There is a fracture through the base of Lewis' odontoid, but it is only slightly displaced on the lateral view and was not at all displaced on the AP view. It can be reduced by traction and will heal with simple support and immobilization.

Marvin Masterstroke (Fig. 121A), the driver, was thrown through the windshield. Instead of a whiplash, he sustained a hard blow to the top of his head. The force was transmitted through the atlanto-occipital articulations forcing the lateral masses (dark arrows) of the atlas outward and bursting them (Fig. 121B). These fractures usually occur through the posterior arches of the atlas and are very difficult to visualize on plain film. The diagnosis is made by noting that the lateral edges of the lateral masses of the atlas don't line up with the lateral masses of C2 (light arrows) on the AP views. This injury is not usually associated with cord damage, and it wasn't here.

Answer to the Problem

Take six weights and put three on each side of the balance. If the balance is level, one of the two weights which were not weighed is heavier, and this will be shown by putting them on the balance next.

If the balance is heavier on one side, discard the weights from the light side and place two of three from the heaviest side on the scale. If it balances, the third weight is the heavy one. If it doesn't balance, the heavier weight is on the scale.

Isadore solved the problem while recovering from his injuries.

Figure 121 B Mechanism of a "burst" fracture of the atlas

Page 199

SECTION XVI

Skull and Facial Fractures

CASES 122, 123, 124, AND 125 THREE MEN IN A FIGHT

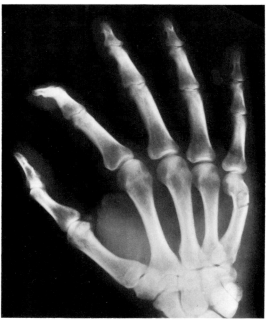

Figure 122   Patrick

Patrick Planter started a fight with **Quentin Queensberry** while they were both enjoying the pleasures of their neighborhood tavern. **Reggie Roustabout** made the mistake of intervening in this altercation. They are all brought to the Emergency Room by their wives who were called by the bartender. Can you sort out their injuries?

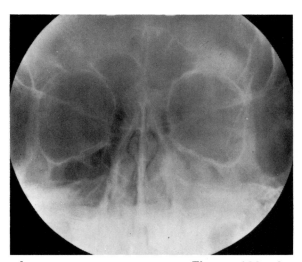

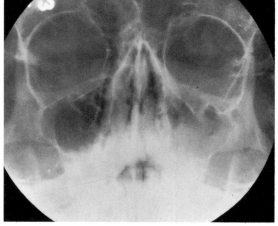

A   **Figure 123 A and B   Quentin**   B

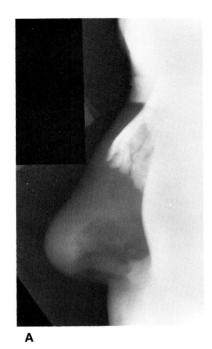

A

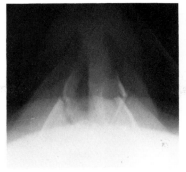

B

**Figure 124   A and B
Reggie**

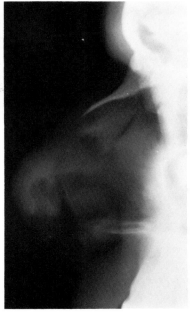

**Figure 124   C
Normal nose**

ANSWER

Patrick (Fig. 122) has fractured the head of his 5th metatarsal—a "boxer's fracture." This fracture is typically angulated slightly in a radial and palmar direction.

Quentin has a "blowout" fracture of his left orbit (Fig. 123A and B). There is fluid in the left maxillary antrum and in the left ethmoid sinus (compare with opposite side, which remains clear). On the Water's view, a depressed fracture of the orbital floor is visible. In this type of injury, the force from the fist is transmitted by the globe and surrounding tissues to the weak "paper plate" of the ethmoid and to the relatively weak orbital floor (roof of the maxillary sinus), causing them both to fracture.

Reggie's intervention has cost him a broken nose (Fig. 124A, B, and C). On the lateral film the fracture fragments are seen to be displaced slightly posteriorly at the tip and, on the inferior view, laterally. Notice the groove of the nasociliary artery and nerve on the normal nose for comparison. These grooves should not be confused with a fracture.

On hearing how much damage Patrick did to her husband, Quentin's wife landed Pat a right to the jaw. Figure 125 is her hand. Her unprofessional sideswipe has cost her a spiral fracture of the base of the 5th metacarpal, another common fracture among brawlers.

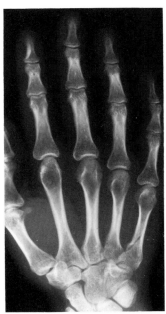

Figure 125   Mrs. Planter

CASES 126, 127, 128, AND 129 MORE FACIAL FRACTURES— ANOTHER FIGHT

Stretch Snodgrass and "Tiger" True-grit are baseball players. Truegrit has hit Stretch in the eye with a wild pitch. Stretch, gone mad, has taken on all comers with his fists and baseball bat. Before being subdued, he landed a right to the cheek of the **Umpire** and almost killed the coach, **Vince Vinnelli,** hitting him across the bridge of his nose with the bat. Truegrit got off lightly with an upper-cut to the jaw. The sorry quartet are brought to see you in the Emergency Room by the Stadium Police. Stretch has double vision, Truegrit a painful jaw, and the Umpire a swollen left cheek. Vince is now conscious, but his face is a mess, and when you pull on his upper teeth there is a sickening lack of rigidity. Can you predict the fractures from the histories?

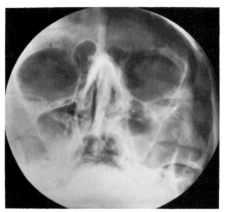

Figure 126 A   Stretch

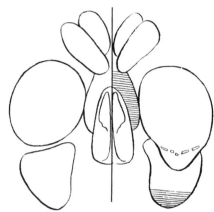

Figure 126 B   Schematic blowout fracture

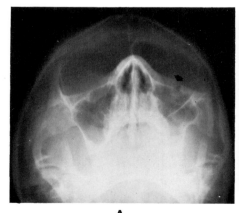

A

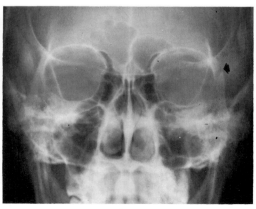

B

Figure 127 A, B, and C   The Umpire: Water's, Caldwell, and base views

ANSWER

Stretch (Fig. 126) has a blowout fracture as was described in Case 123. The Water's view, taken upright, shows the fracture of the floor of the orbit with an air-fluid level in the maxillary antrum. His double vision may be due to limitation of muscle motion and/or displacement of the globe from its normal position by hemorrhage and edema, or to actual entrapment at the inferior rectus muscle in the fracture. Rarely it's due to displacement of the globe caused by the loss of the supporting orbital floor.

The Umpire (Fig. 127A, B, and C) has fractures (arrows) through the maxilla, the frontozygomatic suture, and the zygomatic arch. These three fractures are commonly associated and are called a "tripod fracture." (See schema, Fig. 127D.)

Vincent's fractures (Fig. 128A and B) go through both maxillas, both frontal zygomatic sutures, and the bridge of the nose; that is, bilateral tripods plus a fracture across the nose connecting them. This is a craniofacial separation, attested to by the abnormal mobility of the maxilla.

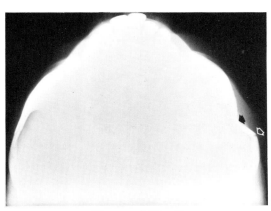

Figure 127   C

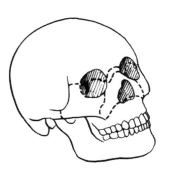

Figure 127   D
Schematic common facial fractures

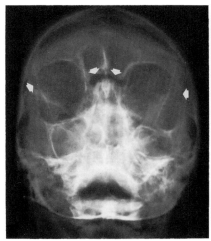

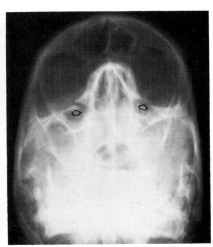

A

B

Figure 128   A and B   The coach

The culprit, **Truegrit,** has fractures through the jaw (Fig. 129A, B, and C). Jaw fractures are characteristically bilateral, unless at the symphysis, and frequently run to the root of a molar, as they do here (arrows). If you see only one fracture on the routine film, look for a second fracture through the mandibular condyles or a dislocation of a temporomandibular joint. As in this case, they are often best seen on oblique views of the mandible and would be missed on conventional facial films.

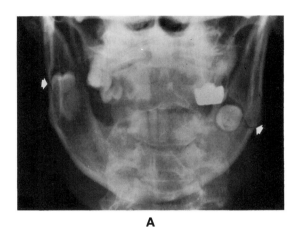

A

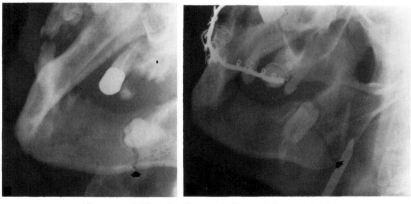

B   **C**

Figure 129   A, B, and C   The culprit

CASES 130, 131, AND 132 STRUCK ON HEAD— RULE OUT SKULL FRACTURE

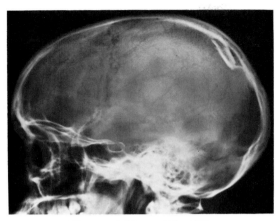

Figure 130   Wycliffe

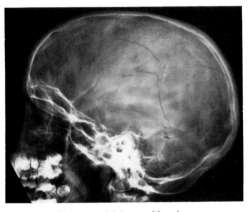

Figure 131   Xavier

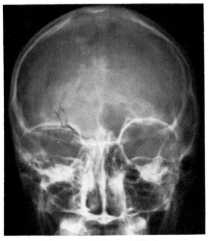

Figure 132   Yale

This is a very common problem. It has been found that skull films are unlikely to influence the treatment of a patient who has no neurologic deficit. Nevertheless, there are some skull fractures which should be treated with caution, even if the patient appears well. Do you recognize them?

Wycliffe Walpurgisnacht, Xavier Xavier, and **Yale Yuccaflatte** have been mixing it up at a protest rally and are brought in by the police. All are claiming police brutality except for Wycliffe, who is a policeman; he is claiming protester brutality.

ANSWER

Wycliffe (Fig. 130) has certainly been assaulted. He has a depressed fracture of his occiput. This needs careful attention because it may be associated with a tear in the dura underneath it, or possibly with a contusion or laceration of the brain. A fracture depressed this far needs to be elevated surgically. Remember, you may only be able to confirm that a skull fracture is depressed with specially tailored tangential views.

Xavier, an 8-year-old (Fig. 131), says he is fine and wants to go home, but you should keep him overnight. Some of the ramifications of that stellate fracture run across the coronal suture and the groove of the middle meningeal artery, which runs just posterior to the suture. The artery or its corresponding vein may have been torn, in which case there may be a developing epidural hematoma.

Yale's fracture (Fig. 132) runs into the right frontal sinus (which is filled with blood). It therefore communicates with the outside. It is a potential route for meningitis. Fractures into any paranasal air sinus, into the middle ear, or through the olfactory plate should all be considered potentially contaminated.

SECTION XVII

Fractures with Associated Soft Tissue Injury

CASES 133 TO 139 FRACTURES COMMONLY ASSOCIATED WITH INJURIES TO ARTERIES OR NERVES

Several common fractures are likely to be associated with damage to neighboring arteries or nerves. Vessel injuries include lacerations, spasm, and thrombus. It is important to recognize the vessel injury. If the bleeding is deep, as in the thigh, it may not be appreciated until the patient goes into shock. Also, vascular spasm and thrombosis must be recognized and corrected within about six hours if irreversible tissue damage is to be avoided. Nerve injuries likewise may range from complete laceration, with possibly irreparable loss of function, to contusion, with only a transient physiologic block to nerve impulses. It is important to identify high-risk fractures and to treat them with care. A vessel or nerve which is still intact may easily be severed during an attempt at reduction of a fracture.

Cases 133A to 139A are common fractures. Can you name these fractures and can you predict which arteries and/or nerves might have been injured? Figures 133B to 139B are composite drawings showing the injuries which might be expected to accompany the fractures.

It should be noted that some fractures are particularly dangerous, since the muscles attached to the fractured fragments pull them against the adjacent vessels or nerve. Supracondylar fractures of the femur and humerus are examples of this phenomenon.

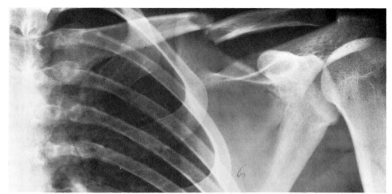

Figure 133   A

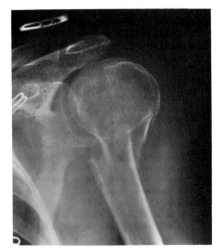

Figure 134   A

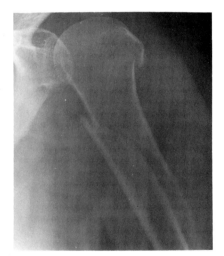

Figure 135   A

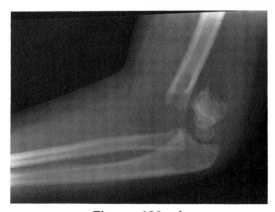

Figure 136   A

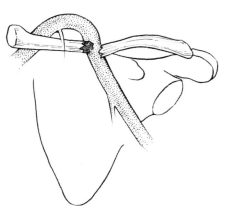

Figure 133 B Fractured clavicle—injury to subclavian artery or nerve

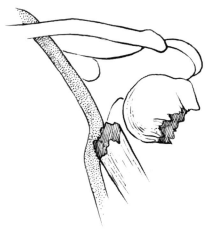

Figure 134 B Surgical neck of humerus—injury to axillary nerve or artery

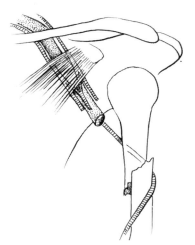

Figure 135 B Middle third of humerus—injury to radial nerve

Figure 136 B Supracondylar fracture of humerus—injury to brachial artery or median nerve

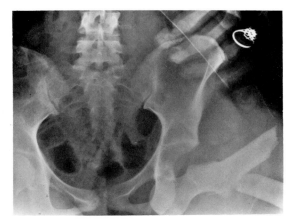

Figure 137 A

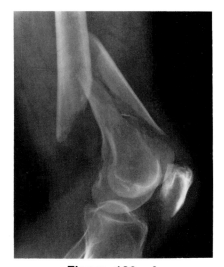

Figure 138 A

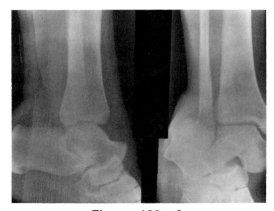

Figure 139 A

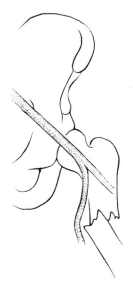

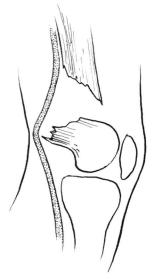

Figure 137 B Femoral fracture — injury to superficial or profunda femoral artery

Figure 138 B Supracondylar fracture of femur — injury to popliteal artery

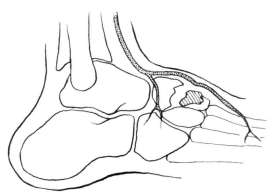

Figure 139 B Fracture dislocation of foot — injury to dorsalis pedis or tibial artery

CASE 140   BLEEDING INTO THE CHEST

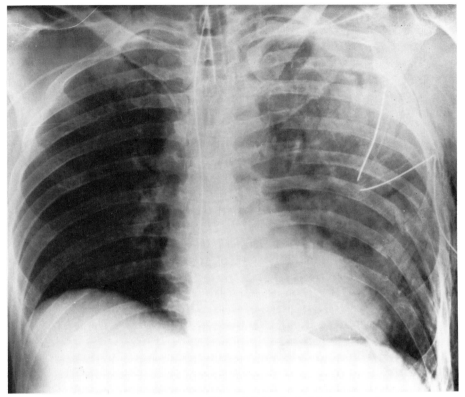

Figure 140   A   "Butch" Bullwinkle's chest

"Butch" Bullwinkle, ace stockcar driver, went off the course into the stands. He has been in the Emergency Room for about three hours now but still requires blood replacement. The plain film of his chest (Fig. 140A) shows fluid (increased density) in the left chest in spite of continuous drainage of blood and pleural fluid from the chest tube. What do you think the source of this bleeding might be?

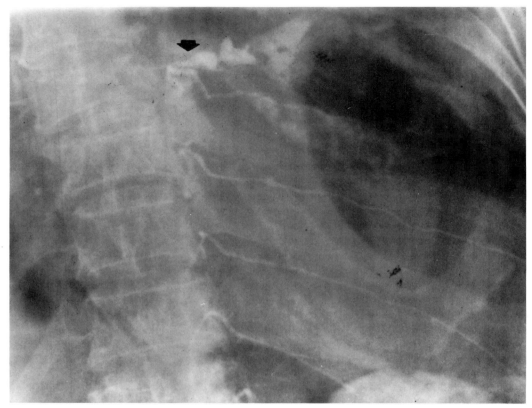

Figure 140   B   A film from his aortogram

ANSWER

The possibilities are lacerations of the aorta, of the intercostal arteries, or, less likely, of a pulmonary artery. The chest film reveals fractures of most of the left ribs posteriorly. Several of these fractures are diastatic, with sharp overlapping fracture ends.

The aortogram was normal, but a later film (Fig. 140B) opacifying the intercostal arteries clearly shows extravasation of contrast from the bleeding intercostal (arrow).

Sometimes the nature of a fracture, particularly the fracture of an extremity, is such that the source of bleeding can be reasonably deduced without an angiogram (Cases 133 to 139). Complex injuries such as this one, however, require angiography or surgical exploration to identify the bleeding site.

CASE 141 PELVIC FRACTURE WITH INTERNAL BLEEDING

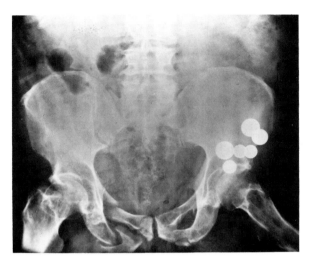

Figure 141 A   Albright's plain film

Anthony Albright, a retired shoe-maker, was making his way across Hay-market Square when he was knocked down by a runaway cart of melons. One wheel of the cart ran over his abdomen. On physical examination his pelvis is painful and unstable. He is in shock, and his hematocrit and blood pressure are not rising even though he has had 4 units of blood. Figures 141A and B are his plain film and an angiogram. Can you spot the bleeding source?

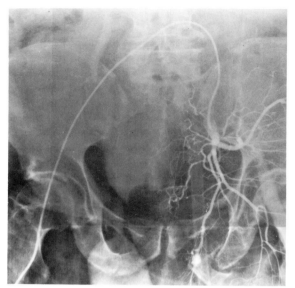

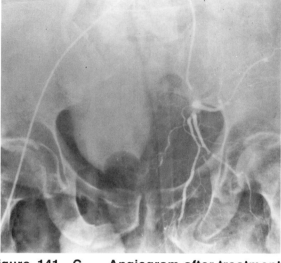

Figure 141　B　The angiogram　　　**Figure 141　C　Angiogram after treatment**

ANSWER

If you haven't seen the bleeding, look at the fractures; they are, as it were, nature's way of telling the angiographer where to put his catheter. There is a teardrop of extravasated contrast near the fractures of the left inferior pubic ramus. The blood is coming from one of the smaller branches of the obturator artery, itself a branch of the hypogastric artery. In spite of the small amount of extravasated blood that is visualized, this is a massive retroperitoneal bleed. Look how the contrast-filled bladder (faint) has been displaced by the pelvic hematoma. This obturator artery will be difficult to approach surgically. Can you think of another way to stop the bleeding?

ANSWER

The angiographers mixed some of the patient's own blood with fibrinogen and then injected the clot into the bleeding artery. Figure 141C is a film obtained subsequently showing that the extravasation has ceased. This method of controlling hemorrhage is feasible as long as the area distal to the vessel to be occluded by clot can be supplied by collateral blood flow (as it can be here).

CASES 142 AND 143 TWO PATIENTS WITH TRAUMA AND HEMATURIA

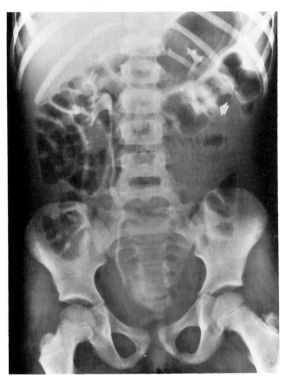

Figure 142   Billy's IVP

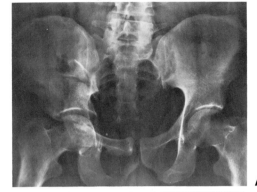

A

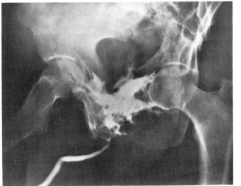

B

Figure 143   A and B   The grandfather's pelvis and the retrograde urethrogram

Billy Budd and **Charles Chiari** have grossly bloody urine following blunt trauma to the abdomen. Budd, a 5-year-old boy, and Chiari, his 55-year-old grandfather, were struck by a car while crossing the street. The boy (Fig. 142, an IVP) was knocked clear and is complaining only of pain and tenderness on palpation of the left upper quadrant and left lower ribs. The grandfather (Fig. 143A) was trapped under the car and has a painful, unstable pelvis. He cannot void but there is a small amount of blood coming from his penis.

ANSWER

Billy's IVP does not show his undisplaced rib fractures, but it does show an amorphous collection of contrast leaking from the inferior calyces of the left kidney (arrow). No contrast enters the ureter. Billy is taken to the operating room and a laceration of the renal pelvis is repaired.

Rib fractures may be a tip-off to underlying renal trauma. Similarly, fractures of transverse processes may be associated with lacerations of the ureters. The fractures themselves may not cause direct damage to the underlying organs, but they are indicators of the site of the trauma.

Mr. Chiari, the grandfather (Fig. 143B), has fractures through his pubic rami. Unable to get a catheter into the bladder, the urologist injected contrast into the distal urethra. The contrast has extravasated from the lacerated prostatic urethra into the surrounding tissues. A later film from an IVP showed that the bladder itself was intact. This lesion was treated by placing a catheter through the wound into the bladder and allowing the epithelium to reconstitute around the catheter.

SECTION XVIII

Blunt Trauma

Blunt trauma is nonpenetrating trauma. Some of the injuries which result from blunt trauma have already been discussed in the section dealing with fractures. However, there may be serious injury without a fracture, particularly in young patients with flexible bones.

It is useful to keep in mind the possible injuries resulting from external violence to the chest or the abdomen. There is often very little time to consider and to make a diagnosis. The radiologist and attending physician must be aware beforehand of the potential internal injuries which threaten the life or affect the management of the patient with blunt trauma to the chest or abdomen. Injuries to be kept in mind include fractures of the ribs, sternum, or spine; pulmonary contusions; pneumothorax; tracheobronchial fractures; aortic, esophageal, or diaphragmatic tears; ruptures of the spleen, liver, or kidney; and hematomas or ruptures of the duodenum and pancreas, or, in some seat-belt injuries, of the intestines.

CASES 144 AND 145   BLUNT CHEST TRAUMA

Fred Felty (Fig. 144A) and **George Gilbert** (Fig. 145A) are the drivers of two cars involved in a head-on collision. Both have multiple abrasions and contusions. What tentative diagnoses will you entertain?

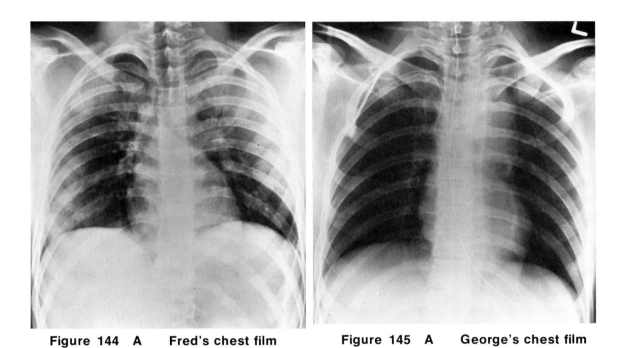

Figure 144 A   Fred's chest film   **Figure 145 A   George's chest film**

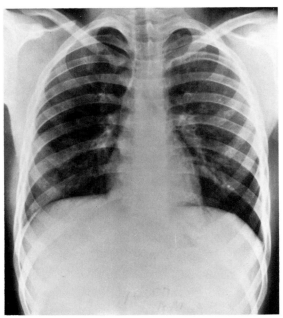

Figure 144 B   Fred's chest two days later

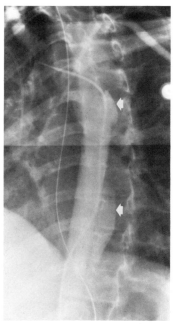

Figure 145 B   George's aortogram

ANSWER

Mr. Felty's chest is normal except for confluent densities in the periphery of his lungs obscuring the normal pulmonary vessels and not corresponding to a segmental distribution. As noted previously, this is a nonspecific pattern simply indicating fluid of some type in the alveoli. In this setting pulmonary contusion with hemorrhage in the alveoli is a good possibility. The rapid clearing in 48 hours (Fig. 144B) is typical. These patients may be dyspneic but may be completely asymptomatic. Hemoptysis is only an occasional symptom.

Mr. Gilbert's heart, lungs, and thorax are normal, but the aorta is not; its margin is indistinct. That blurring is due to blood leaking from the aorta into the adventitia which surrounds the aorta. A laceration of a small mediastinal vessel might produce the same appearance on a chest film, but the aortogram (Fig. 145B) shows contrast leaking from tears in the lumen of the descending aorta (arrows). The diagnosis is thus confirmed.

CASES 146 AND 147 TWO MORE MEN FROM A
HEAD-ON COLLISION

Henry Horner and **Harold Hurler** are the passengers from the same cars driven by Mr. Felty and Mr. Gilbert. They are both severely dyspneic, but neither is in shock. Can you tell what has happened to them?

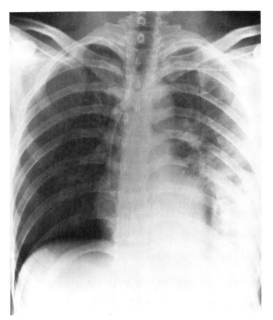

Figure 146 A   Horner's chest film

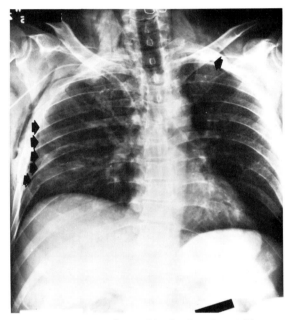

Figure 147 A   Hurler's chest film

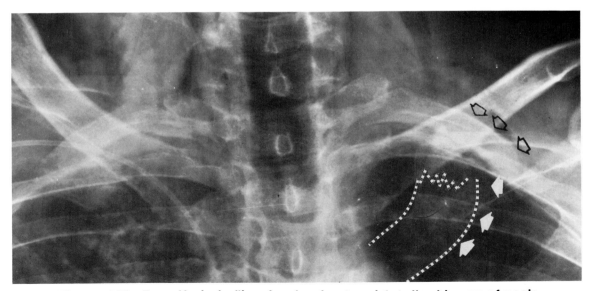

Figure 147 B   Hurler's film showing fractured 1st rib—blowup of neck

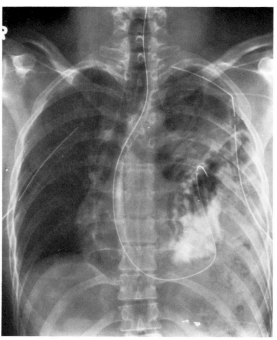

Figure 146 B   Horner's chest film with contrast in the stomach

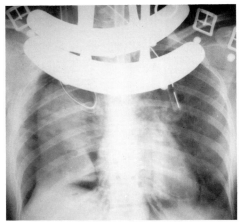

Figure 147 C   A severed bronchus

ANSWER

Mr. Horner's chest film is grossly abnormal. The left hemidiaphragm is not seen and there is an amorphous irregular density in the left lower chest.

Suspecting the possibility of diaphragmatic rupture, the house officer has passed a nasogastric tube. The radiologist then injected a small amount of water-soluble contrast into the nasogastric tube, confirming that the stomach was intact but herniated through the ruptured diaphragm into the chest.

Mr. Hurler's chest film is harder to interpret (Fig. 147A and B). There is extensive subcutaneous and mediastinal emphysema, a small right pneumothorax (short arrows), and fractures of the first rib (long arrows) as well as of several other ribs. This triad should make you consider the diagnosis of a *fractured bronchus*. Most patients with rib fractures and small pneumothoraces do not have extensive mediastinal emphysema, since the usual post-traumatic pneumothorax is due to rupture of the peripheral pleura rather than to a mediastinal tear. These rib fractures are significant, since 90% of patients with bronchial fractures have fracture of the first three ribs. The diagnosis should also be considered in any patient with severe blunt chest trauma whose pneumothorax does not respond to suction. In Mr. Hurler's case, the diagnosis was confirmed at bronchoscopy. Case 147C is a different patient in whom the right mainstem bronchus has been *completely severed*, allowing the collapsing lung to fall *away* from the mediastinum instead of collapsing toward it, as it must do when held in place by the main bronchus.

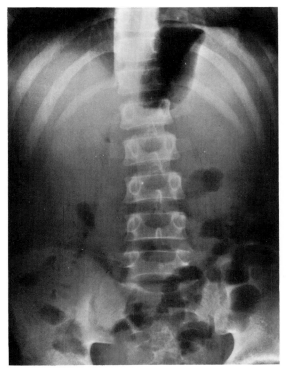

Figure 148   A   Kathy's plain film

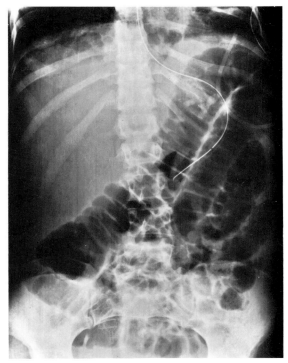

Figure 149   A   Kelly's plain film

Katherine Kartagener (Fig. 148A) and **Kelly Klinefelter** (Fig. 149A) were driving home from a party when their car went out of control and hit an abutment. Neither girl has any fractures, but both have abdominal pain and nausea. Kathy has pain in the tip of her left shoulder. Shortly afterwards Kelly complains of right shoulder pain. Both girls have epigastric tenderness and guarding, but bowel sounds are present. Their hematocrits are normal and there is no blood in the urine. Do the symptoms and plain films of the abdomen suggest diagnoses to you?

ANSWER

Kathy's spleen is enlarged, extending down into the abdomen and displacing the stomach bubble medially. Kelly's liver looks big too, but liver size is much more difficult to estimate. Both have pain suggesting subdiaphragmatic irritation. What do you make of their angiograms (Fig. 148B and 149B)?

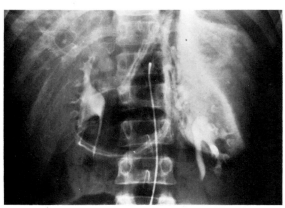

Figure 148 B   Kathy's angiogram

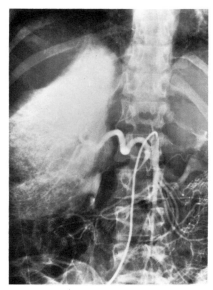

Figure 149 B   Kelly's angiogram

ANSWER

Kathy's spleen is compressed by a lenticular mass which does not opacify with contrast: a subcapsular hematoma of the spleen. Kelly has a large sub- capsular hematoma of the liver. Both girls were taken to surgery. If these hematomas break through the capsule, there could be sudden massive intra- abdominal hemorrhage.

CASE 150   A SEAT-BELT INJURY

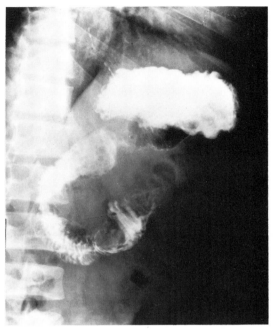

Figure 150   A   Larry Loeffler's upper gastrointestinal series

Larry Loeffler, a 26-year-old intoxicated graduate student, was driving home from a party when he struck a parked car. He was wearing a lap-type seat belt, and his upper abdomen struck the steering wheel. He is brought to your Emergency Room by the State Police.

Larry's vital signs are normal as are his hematocrit and urinalysis, but his epigastrium is extremely tender. Shortly after admission he begins to vomit bile-stained liquid, which is trace guaiac-positive. His amylase is twice normal. His plain film of the abdomen is normal. Figure 150A is a 30-minute film from an upper G.I. series. What is your diagnosis?

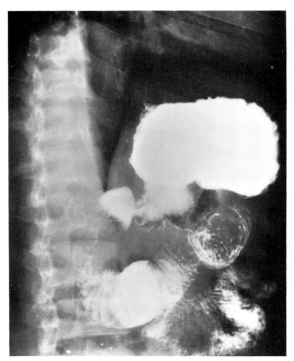

Figure 150 B His duodenum one week later

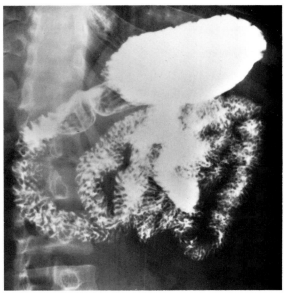

Figure 150 C Two months later

ANSWER

At 30 minutes, barium should have passed through the duodenum; there must be an obstruction of some sort. The tip-off to the cause of the obstruction is thickening and distortion of the folds in the duodenum, with a mass apparently effacing the folds entirely in one area near the blockage.

These are the findings of an intramural hematoma of the retroperitoneal portion of the duodenum, the most common *intestinal* injury resulting from blunt abdominal trauma. Figures 150B and C are Larry's films from a week later

and 2 months later showing the gradual resolution of the hematoma. The one-week film shows the "coiled spring" appearance of the mucosa infiltrated with hematoma. This is not a surgical lesion. Frank rupture of the duodenum would, of course, require surgery.

Did you consider the diagnosis of a pancreatic laceration or hemorrhage? It is a reasonable diagnosis, and we weren't trying to be tricky with that amylase. A slightly elevated amylase is common in duodenal hematomas. In a pancreatic laceration the amylase would characteristically be many times normal (though it might be low initially).

SECTION XIX

Headache

Most of us have headaches at one time or another and do not think anything of it. Patients who come to the Emergency Room with headaches are relatively uncommon. When they do present themselves, they should be taken seriously.

It is very difficult to evaluate the intensity of pain, especially headache pain. Other symptoms or signs must be sought. Headaches which keep the patient awake at night, which are associated with nausea and vomiting, or which are associated with tachycardia or sweating are usually organic in nature. Headaches associated with neurologic deficit, of course, are almost always due to an organic lesion.

The common severe headaches seen in the Emergency Room are migraine, sinusitis, and "tension" headaches. Subdural hematoma and meningitis are less common, though both may present without neurologic deficit or history of trauma. Brain tumors, of course, are rare.

Skull films are infinitely less valuable in the evaluation of headache than are a complete history and physical examination. However, the skull film may confirm a diagnosis or exclude a diagnosis in some instances, and the clinician should be aware at least of the clues which may be found on a skull film.

The following patients come to the Emergency Room because of intractable headache. **Mary Maffucci** (Fig. 151A to D) is in good health, but **Peter Pickwick** (Fig. 152A and B) has a fever and pain on the right side of his nose and behind the right eye. What do you make of their films?

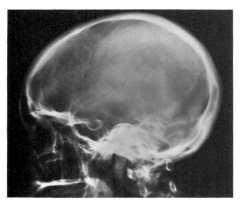

A   Lateral view

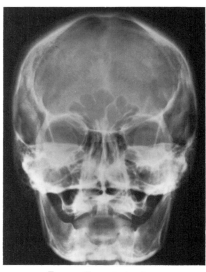

B   Frontal view

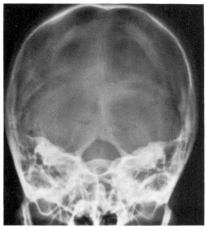

C   Towne's or occipital view

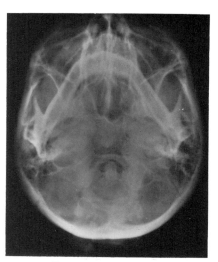

D   Base view

Figure 151   Mary Maffucci's skull films

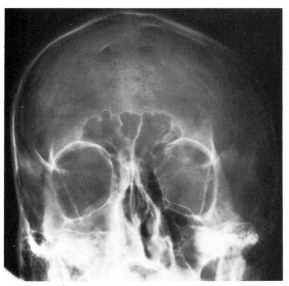
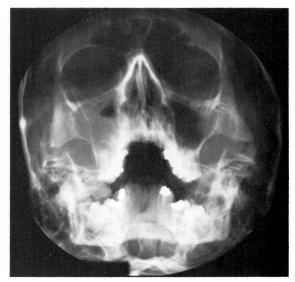

A   **Figure 152   A and B**   **Peter Pickwick's sinus films**   **B**

ANSWER

Mary's skull films are normal: the calvarium is intact; the sutures and vascular grooves are normal in caliber; the sella is well mineralized and of normal size; the paranasal air sinuses are well aerated and the surrounding bones intact. (The pineal is not seen.) Further history reveals that Mary got a new pair of reading glasses last week. Upon reflection she dates her headache from this time.

Peter's films are not normal, are they? The upright Water's view of his face shows an air-fluid level in his right maxillary antrum. The frontal or "Caldwell" view show that the right ethmoid sinus is not aerated either. Peter has right maxillary and ethmoidal sinusitis.

This history is acute, and the surrounding bone margins are sharp. It is safe to assume that this is an acute pyogenic infection. It must be treated promptly, though, or there will be danger of osteomyelitis or of a spreading infection, including meningitis. Sinus pain is well localized except for sphenoid sinus pain, which is roughly central in the head. An acutely blocked sinus produces severe intractable pain, often associated with high fever.

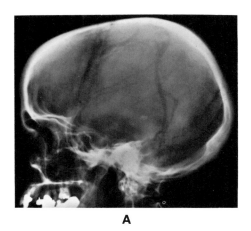

A

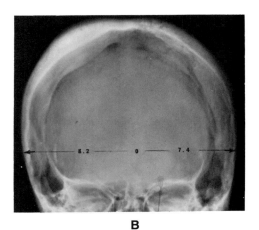

B

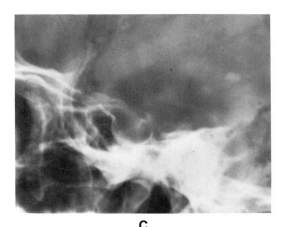

C

Figure 153 A, B, and C   Richard's AP and lateral skull films

The next two patients are more seriously ill. **Richard Reiter** (Fig. 153A to C) has had a headache for a year, and on physical examination his left side is weaker than his right, though he had not noticed this himself. **Sven Sjögren** (Fig. 154A and B), an 8-year-old child, is drowsy and has had a stumbling gait for about two weeks.

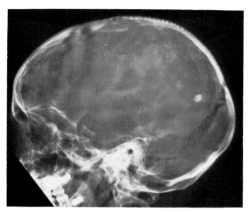

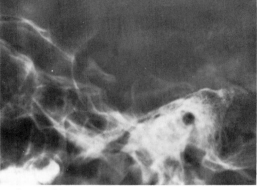

A   **Figure 154   A and B   Sven Sjogren**   B

ANSWER

Richard's skull film is unusually dramatic: there is thickening (hyperostosis) of bone in the right posterior parietal area, enlargement of the sella, and displacement of the pineal inferiorly and to the left by about 4 mm. (Maximum permissible shift in an *asymptomatic* patient is 2 mm from the midline. In the presence of lateralizing signs, any shift is significant.) In addition, the grooves of the middle meningeal vessels near the coronal sutures are abnormally wide, and there is an abnormal vascular groove in the parietal region. These are the findings of a meningioma: local hyperostosis, enlargement of the meningeal vessels and draining veins, a mass effect displacing the pineal, and secondary changes in the sella due to chronically increased intracranial pressure.

Little **Sven** has two additional findings: abnormal intracranial calcifications (in the tumor) and separation of his (unfused) cranial sutures. He has an enlarged and eroded sella too. Sven's tumor was a glioma which was inoperable, unfortunately.

CASE 155 LONG-TERM INCREASED INTRACRANIAL PRESSURE

Richard and Sven were presented to show the dramatic changes which may be present in the skull of the patient with a brain tumor (Cases 153 and 154). More commonly, even with a brain tumor, the skull film will be normal. If you are lucky you may see the less striking but relatively common abnormality that **Terry Tietze's** case illustrates (Fig. 155A, B, and C).

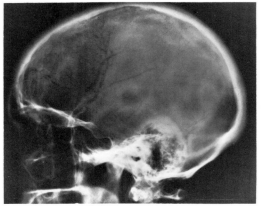
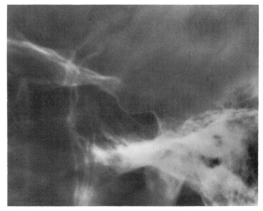

A   Figure 155   A and B   Terry Tietze   **B**

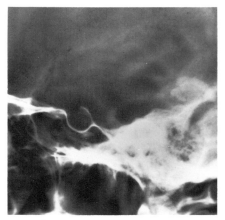

Figure 155   C   Terry's sella before the tumor

ANSWER

Terry's skull is normal except for severe demineralization of the dorsum sellae. The early view of Terry's sella is normal (Fig. 155C). Now, the dorsum, especially the inside of the dorsum, has been demineralized and eroded away in response to increased pressure in the subarachnoid space. The thicker cortex of the back of the sella and the reinforcing cortex of the sphenoid sinus make the rest of the sella relatively resistant to demineralization. That is why we look for the earliest changes in the inside of the dorsum.

SECTION XX

Head Trauma and Coma

A great many diseases, toxins, and traumas may render a patient unconscious: diabetes, hepatic failure, cardiac arrhythmias, meningitis, brain tumors, alcohol, sedatives, and so on. The role of skull films is mainly limited to a search for skull fractures, pineal shift, demineralization of the sella, and evidence of tumor or infection in the base of the skull as has been noted previously.

If there are no focal neurologic signs, and if the spinal fluid is normal, further radiologic examination of the brain is not usually undertaken. In the presence of focal neurologic deficit, especially lateralizing signs, cerebral angiography is frequently useful. Three common causes of coma with neurologic deficit are subdural hematoma, epidural hematoma, and cerebrovascular accidents including intracerebral hemorrhage.

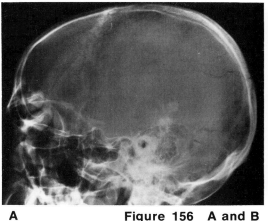
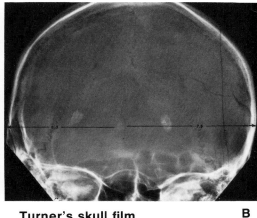

A   Figure 156   A and B   Turner's skull film   B

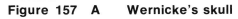

Figure 157   A   Wernicke's skull

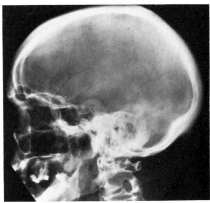

Figure 158   A   Major Wolff-Parkinson-White's skull

The next three patients are brought to the Emergency Room unconscious, with signs referable to the left cerebral cortex. **Timothy Turner** (Fig. 156A and B) is an alcoholic who was last admitted to the Emergency Room a month ago for seizures, at which time an occipital skull fracture was noted. However, his skull film was otherwise normal except for an incidental finding of calcification of the choroid plexus in the lateral ventricles. The pineal was midline. A brain scan was normal. He was discharged after 48 hours of observation.

William Wernicke (Fig. 157A and B) is also an alcoholic. He was found unconscious at the bottom of a flight of stairs.

Warren Wolff-Parkinson-White (Fig. 158A, B, and C) is a Major in the Salvation Army. He was found unconscious in a slum. His blood pressure is 180/120.

What do you make of the plain films of the skull? We will show you the carotid angiograms in a moment.

ANSWER

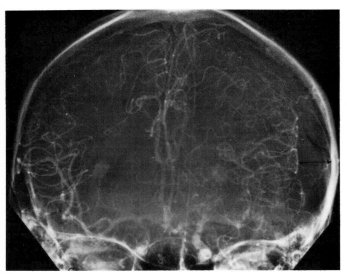

Figure 156 C   Turner's carotid angiogram

Turner's skull film has changed. The pineal and choroid plexus calcifications have been shifted to the right about 6 mm. Figure 156C is Turner's carotid angiogram showing the vessels of the surface of the brain separated from the inner table of the skull by 15 mm. This is a subdural hematoma, probably the result of the old fracture and probably present, but much smaller, at the time of the previous admission. The hematoma has absorbed fluid in the intervening time and has enlarged until it now causes symptoms. It was drained surgically.

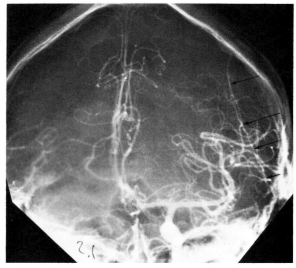

Figure 157 B   Wernicke's angiogram

Wernicke's skull fracture is more worrisome than was Timothy's. It crosses the groove of the middle meningeal artery just behind the coronal suture. Furthermore, Wernicke has symptoms of a lesion involving the cerebral cortex underneath the fracture. His angiogram (Fig. 157B) is more complicated to interpret but distinctly abnormal. That curvilinear vessel (arrows) is not one of the sylvian (cortical) vessels; it is coming up from the base of the skull. The displaced vessel is the middle meningeal artery lateral to the sylvian vessels, displaced by an *epidural* hemorrhage caused by a laceration of the middle meningeal artery at the time of the fracture.

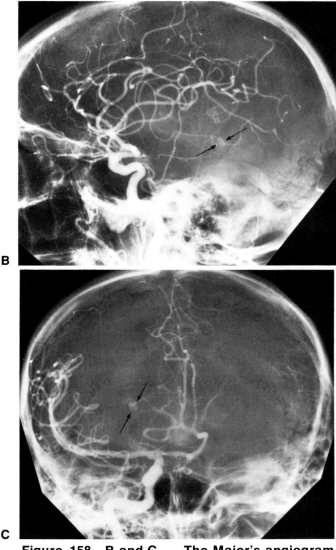

B

C

Figure 158   B and C   The Major's angiogram

Major White's skull films are normal, but his angiogram (Fig. 158B and C) is not. There is a leak of blood from the anterior choroidal artery with a puddle of contrast on his angiogram, an intra-cerebral hemorrhage, due to his hypertension. Major White was treated with antihypertensive medication and recovered almost completely.

INDEX

INDEX

INDEX

INDEX

Gallbladder, emphysematous cholecystitis, 93–94
  hydrops, 75–76
  ruptured, 94
Gastric obstruction, 143–144
Gastric ulcer, 126–127
Gastritis, angiography and, 128–130
Gastroenteritis, 67–68

Hand, foreign body in, 173
  fracture of, 200, 201
Head trauma, and coma, 233–237
Headache, 227–232
Hematemesis, 119–130
Hematoma, epidural, 235–236
  of duodenum, 225–226
  of liver, 223–224
  of spleen, 223–224
  subdural, 235–236
Hemoptysis, 53–64
Hemorrhage, intracerebral, 235, 237
Heroin, pulmonary edema and, 41–42
Hyperemesis gravidarum, 158–159
Hypotension, abdominal pain and, 87–101

Ileus, gallstone, 105–106
Impaction, fecal, 117–118
Infarction, mesenteric, 97–98, 137–138
  myocardial, 3–4, 11
  pulmonary evolution of, 43–44
Ingestion(s), acid, 162
  hydrocarbons, 163–164
  lye, 165–166
  poisonings and, 161–166
Intestinal obstruction, in pregnancy, 158–159
  large bowel, 111–114
  small bowel, 103–104
Intracerebral hemorrhage, 235, 237
Intussusception, 109–110

Jaw, fracture of, 204

Kidney, rupture of, 215–216

Lead poisoning, 81–82
Liver, hematoma of, 223–224
Lung scan, 10, 44, 58

Megacolon, toxic, 135–136
Mesenteric infarction, 97–98, 137–138
Mitral stenosis, 61–62
Myocardial infarction, 3–4, 11

Nose, fracture of, 201

Obstetric radiology, 151–159
Obstruction, gastric, 143–144
  intestinal, in pregnancy, 158–159
    large bowel, 111–114
    small bowel, 103–104

Pancreatitis, 73–74, 91–92
Pelvis, fracture of, with arterial injury, 213–214
Pericardial effusion, 15–16

Pneumonia, cavitating, 63–64
  kerosene, 163–164
  Klebsiella, 51–52
  lobar, 45–46
  viral, 47–48
Pneumothorax, 7–8
  tension, 25–26
Poisoning, ingestions and, 161–166
  lead, 81–82
Pregnancy, 142
  abdominal, 154–155
  anencephaly, 157
  breech, 151, 152
  early signs of, 159
  fetal death, 156
  intestinal obstruction and, 158–159
  placenta praevia, 153
  vertex, 151, 152
Pulmonary angiography, 37–38, 57–58
Pulmonary edema, 20–22
  heroin use and, 41–42
  interstitial, 5–6
Pulmonary embolism, 9–10, 57–58
  angiography and, 37–38, 57–58
Pulmonary infarction, evolution of, 43–44
Pulmonary scan, 10, 44, 58

Rectum, foreign body in, 172
Renal emphysema, 99–100
Ribs, fracture of, 11, 23–24
    with arterial injury, 211–212

Schatzki ring, 147–148
Shock, abdominal pain and, 87–101
Shoulder, fracture of, 188–189
Sinusitis, 228–229
Skull, fracture of, 205
Spine, cervical, fracture of, 196–199
  injuries to, 193–199
  lumbar, injuries to, 194–195
Spleen, hematoma of, 223–224
Stenosis, mitral, 61–62
Sternum, fracture of, 17
Stomach, foreign body in, 171
Subdural hematoma, 235–236

Toxic megacolon, 135–136
Trachea, foreign body in, 168
Trauma, blunt, 217–226
  head, and coma, 233–237

Ulcer, duodenal, 71–72
  angiography and, 121–122
  perforated, 89–90
  gastric, 126–127
Ulcerative colitis, 133–134
Ureteral calculus, 79–80
Urethra, rupture of, 215–216

Varices, esophageal, angiography and, 123–125
Volvulus, cecal, 107–108
  sigmoid, 115–116
Vomiting, 141–150

Wrist, fracture of, 182–187